KRISTEN PARKER

A Love Held in the Hollow Echo

Contents

One

The Echo's Call

The wind whispered through the cracked stones like a forgotten lullaby, carrying with it a sense of unease. Veyrina Lioris stood at the edge of the shattered temple, her fingers brushing against the weathered surface of the ancient ruins. The air felt thick, heavy with something unspoken, like a truth she couldn't grasp no matter how hard she tried. The pull was faint at first—an insistent tug in the depths of her chest that felt like a half-remembered dream. But now, it was impossible to ignore. The echo was growing louder.

The landscape before her was desolate—an endless stretch of broken earth, where twisted trees with pale bark clung to the ground like brittle skeletons. There was no sky, no horizon, just a heavy, perpetual twilight that made everything seem suspended in time. The colors were muted, as if the world itself had forgotten how to live, frozen in a moment that had lasted far too long. In this place, time did not flow.

Veyrina inhaled deeply, feeling the weight of the silence pressing down on her. She had traveled far, searching for something she couldn't quite name. Something had drawn her to this place, a pull she couldn't ignore, and now it was overwhelming her, guiding her deeper into the heart of the forgotten realm. She didn't know why she had come, only that the echo called to her, pulling her toward it like a moth to a flame.

Her eyes scanned the ruins before her. The broken columns and shattered stones seemed to pulse with an ancient energy, a faint hum reverberating in the air. She stepped forward, her boots crunching against the earth, the sound amplified in the unnerving silence. Her heart raced, and she felt the strange pull deep inside her, urging her to move closer.

At the center of the ruins, half-buried beneath a pile of debris, something glimmered in the dim light. It was small, barely visible, but there was no mistaking the sense of urgency in the echo. She approached it cautiously, her fingers trembling as she brushed the stones aside. Her breath caught in her throat as the object came into view—a relic, an artifact of some kind. It was round and smooth, its surface etched with intricate patterns that seemed to shift before her eyes, as if the very markings were alive.

The moment her fingers made contact with the artifact, the pull in her chest intensified, flooding her senses with a rush of emotions—strange, unfamiliar memories flashing through her mind like fractured images. Faces she didn't recognize, places she'd never been, all blending together in a dizzying swirl. Her vision blurred, and for a moment, she thought she might lose herself to it, drowning in the weight of the memories that were not her own.

Then, just as suddenly as it had started, it stopped. The pull diminished, leaving her breathless and disoriented. She pulled her hand away from the artifact, her heart still pounding in her chest, but the echo didn't fade. It lingered, louder now, as if beckoning her further into the heart of the ruins.

A voice broke the silence.

"You should not have touched that."

Veyrina froze, her heart leaping in her chest. The voice was soft, melodic, and yet it carried an edge of warning, a sharpness that sent a chill down her spine. She spun around, searching for the source, but saw no one. The ruins around her stood empty, save for the shattered remnants of the forgotten temple. And yet… she wasn't alone.

"Who's there?" she called out, her voice trembling slightly.

From the shadows, a figure emerged—a woman, tall and graceful, her movements fluid as if she were a part of the very twilight that enveloped the realm. Her features were striking, her skin pale as moonlight, her hair long and dark, falling in waves around her shoulders. But it was her eyes that drew Veyrina in—silver-gray, luminous, as if they held the secrets of the world within them.

"You shouldn't be here," the woman continued, her gaze never leaving Veyrina's face. "This is not a place for the living."

Veyrina took an instinctive step back, the pulse of the echo still echoing in her chest, growing louder, more insistent. The woman's words struck her like a blow, but it was the echo that held her in place, anchoring her to the spot.

"Who are you?" Veyrina asked, her voice barely above a whisper. There was something hauntingly familiar about the woman, something she couldn't place, something that stirred deep within her.

The woman's eyes softened, a flicker of recognition flashing across her face. "I am Elyndra Varell."

The name reverberated in Veyrina's mind like a distant bell, ringing with a deep resonance she couldn't understand. She had heard it before—had she?—but the memories were as elusive as the realm itself.

"Veyrina Lioris," she whispered to herself, as though testing the name. But it felt strange on her tongue, as if it didn't belong to her. The echo tugged at her again, drawing her toward Elyndra as though their fates were bound together by some unseen force.

Elyndra took a step closer, her expression unreadable. "I've been waiting for you."

Veyrina blinked, confusion clouding her thoughts. "Waiting for me? I don't even know you." The words felt like a lie, but she couldn't shake the feeling that she had known this woman once before, in a time that no longer seemed to exist.

"You don't remember," Elyndra said softly, almost as if she were speaking to herself. "But you will. In time."

Veyrina's heart thudded painfully in her chest, the pull of the echo intensifying as Elyndra's words echoed in her mind. She didn't understand, couldn't comprehend the strange connection between them. But she could feel it—this was no accident, no coincidence. She had been drawn here for a reason, and Elyndra Varell was part of that reason.

"What is this place?" Veyrina asked, her voice barely steady. "Where am I?"

Elyndra's gaze softened, a flicker of sadness passing through her eyes. "This is a forgotten land, a realm outside of time. A place where memories are trapped, where echoes of lives lived linger, lost in the darkness. This is where the past and future collide."

Veyrina's brow furrowed in confusion. "Echoes of lives lived? What are you talking about?"

Elyndra's gaze became distant, as though she were seeing something beyond the ruins, something beyond Veyrina herself. "You and I," she said quietly, "we are bound by a love that time has forgotten. This place is the echo of that love. It calls to us, and it will not let us go."

Veyrina took a step back, her chest tightening. The echo was louder now, pulsing with an urgency that mirrored her own racing heart. She could feel it—something ancient, something powerful, and something terrifying. She could feel the weight of her past, a past that was slipping through her fingers like sand.

"How do you know all of this?" she demanded, her voice tinged with frustration. "How do you know me?"

Elyndra's expression darkened, her lips pressing into a thin line. "Because I remember. I remember everything." She looked down at the artifact in Veyrina's hand. "That is the key. The key to unlocking what was lost. But you must be careful. The echo doesn't give up its secrets easily."

Veyrina felt the weight of the artifact in her hand once more, its markings shifting and writhing as though alive. The echo pulsed stronger, pulling at her very soul. She didn't understand what was happening, but she knew one thing for certain: she was inextricably tied to this place, to Elyndra, and to the mysterious force that had led her here.

The wind picked up, howling through the ruins like a chorus of voices long forgotten. The echo grew louder, and in that moment, Veyrina understood. She wasn't here by chance. She had been drawn here, as had Elyndra, to uncover the secrets of a love lost in time. And together, they would have to face whatever dangers the echo held, or risk being lost to it forever.

The whisper on the wind beckoned again, and Veyrina stepped forward, her hand tightening around the artifact. "I'm ready," she said, her voice steady with a newfound resolve. "Show me the truth."

Elyndra's silver-gray eyes met hers, a flicker of something—hope, fear, longing—shining in their depths. "The truth is waiting for you. But be warned, Veyrina. Some truths are more dangerous than others."

And with that, the realm began to shift around them, the ruins vibrating with an ancient energy, as the echo's call became the only sound that mattered.

The atmosphere thickened, swirling with an intensity that mirrored the growing tension in Veyrina's chest. The ground beneath her feet trembled slightly, as if the very realm itself was aware of her presence, waiting for something to shift. Elyndra's presence, once like an enigma, now seemed to hold the answers to questions that Veyrina couldn't yet frame in her mind. Her heart beat faster as she stood at the precipice of something vast—something ancient.

Elyndra's silver-gray eyes shimmered with an intensity that made the air feel even heavier. "Come, we must leave this place," she said, her voice a quiet whisper that seemed to resonate in the ruins themselves. "Time here is not like it is in the world you know. Every moment is stretched thin. It is better if we move before the echo claims us fully."

Veyrina's breath caught in her throat. She didn't want to leave—didn't want to move away from the artifact that now hummed with an ominous pulse, but Elyndra's words had an undeniable weight. She had to follow. The realm was changing, vibrating as if it were a living thing that reacted to every thought, every movement. The deeper she ventured, the more it seemed to respond, becoming almost sentient.

Without another word, Elyndra led Veyrina through the broken temple's archways, the labyrinthine corridors winding around them like a maze. They passed through stone doors that had long since fallen into disrepair, stepping over debris that crumbled beneath their feet like the dust of ages. Veyrina noticed that as they moved, the echoes grew louder—more distinct. Faint whispers swirled in the air, impossible to understand but undeniable in their presence.

The pull of the echo in her chest remained, thrumming deep

within her, growing stronger with every step. It was as though something—or someone—was calling her from far beyond the walls of this forgotten realm. Something that she couldn't escape, no matter how hard she tried.

As they moved deeper, the architecture shifted. The walls, once cracked and broken, seemed to take on a life of their own, with strange carvings that shifted and reformed before Veyrina's eyes. It was as though the realm itself was alive, breathing, watching. She shuddered involuntarily, feeling the weight of the ancient magic that flowed like a current through the very air they breathed.

"Where are we going?" Veyrina asked, her voice barely more than a murmur.

"To the heart of the echo," Elyndra replied, not missing a step. "Where it all began. The truth of your past is there, waiting to be remembered."

Veyrina felt a surge of unease at the words. The truth of her past? How could she possibly understand any of this? She had no memories—nothing but fragments, fleeting visions that teased her just beyond the reach of her understanding. And yet… and yet, the pull in her chest grew stronger, insistent, urging her forward, urging her to follow the path that Elyndra laid before her.

They rounded a final corner, and Veyrina's breath caught as they entered a vast chamber. The space before her was expansive—far larger than the ruined temple they had passed through. The walls were lined with ancient murals, each one depicting scenes that seemed familiar yet foreign to her— figures locked in eternal embrace, standing against the tide of time itself. The room was illuminated by a pale, otherworldly glow that emanated from the center of the space, casting long, ghostly shadows that danced across the walls.

At the center of the room stood a pedestal, and on it, a single object—glimmering, beckoning, calling.

Veyrina's heart raced as she approached it, her footsteps slow and deliberate, as though she feared that the moment she touched it, everything would change. The artifact from earlier pulsed in her hand, as though it were connected to this new object, as though they were two halves of the same whole.

Elyndra stopped a few paces away, her face shadowed by a deep sorrow that Veyrina couldn't quite place. "It is here," she said softly, her voice barely audible over the echoing hum of the room. "This is where it all began. Where we were lost."

Veyrina's gaze never left the pedestal. She felt herself drawn to it, the echo singing louder in her ears. Her fingers trembled as she reached out, instinct guiding her. The moment her fingers brushed against the surface of the object, the world around her seemed to ripple, as though time itself had fractured.

The air grew thick with energy, and the walls of the chamber seemed to close in on her. The whispers—the echoes—rose to a deafening crescendo, and Veyrina's vision blurred as a surge of memories crashed into her mind.

Her knees buckled, and she collapsed to the floor, gasping for breath. The echoes overwhelmed her senses, and for a moment, she could see nothing but flashes of images—faces, landscapes, moments that were not hers. But there was one face—one presence—that stood out above all others: Elyndra.

And then, everything stopped.

Veyrina's breath came in ragged gasps as she forced herself to sit up, her mind still spinning from the onslaught of memories. She blinked rapidly, trying to focus, trying to make sense of the torrent that had just flooded her mind. But the one thing that remained clear—unshakable—was the connection between her and Elyndra.

She looked up, and there stood the woman, her expression unreadable, her eyes filled with something ancient—something older than time itself.

"You remember now," Elyndra said softly, her voice tinged with sadness. "The love we shared. The love that was lost."

Veyrina's heart skipped a beat as her hand moved instinctively to her chest. She felt the echo in her soul, the resonance of something long forgotten, now awakened.

But there was something else. A shadow behind the memories, a presence that hadn't been there before. A coldness, an unfamiliar feeling that gnawed at the edges of her consciousness.

"What happened to us?" Veyrina asked, her voice trembling.

Elyndra's gaze flickered with something darker. "We were torn apart by forces beyond our control. A curse, a betrayal. The echo you hear now is the remnants of our love, echoing through time, waiting for us to reclaim it."

Veyrina shook her head, confusion and fear overwhelming her. "But I don't understand. I don't remember... I can't remember..."

Elyndra knelt before her, her eyes softening. "That is because time has erased you, Veyrina. Time has hidden the truth from you. But you are not meant to forget. Not anymore. The echo will guide us, but we must face what lies at the heart of it."

A flicker of movement caught Veyrina's eye. A shadow, darting across the far corner of the chamber, a figure cloaked in darkness, half-hidden by the fading light.

"Someone's here," Veyrina whispered, a chill running down

her spine.

Elyndra's eyes widened in recognition. "We are not alone."

Before Veyrina could respond, the figure stepped into the dim light. A man—tall, cloaked in shadows, his features obscured by the darkness. His eyes glowed with an unnatural light, and a cold smile twisted his lips.

"You have awakened it," he said, his voice a low, almost melodic tone. "And now, the price must be paid."

Veyrina's heart raced as the echo pulsed, louder than ever. The air around her seemed to crackle with energy, and she realized, with a chilling certainty, that this was only the beginning. The price was coming, and it was more than she could have ever imagined.

Fragments of a Past

T he cold stone beneath Veyrina's feet seemed to vibrate with a life of its own, every step a resonance that pulsed through her like an echo of something long buried. She had no words for what she felt, no understanding of how she could be so connected to this place—this realm—and yet, with each moment that passed, it felt as though the veil over her memories was being slowly, agonizingly lifted.

Elyndra moved beside her, her presence both a comfort and a mystery. There was a silence between them now, heavier than before, like the weight of something unspoken. Something unfinished. Veyrina could feel it in the way their shoulders brushed ever so slightly as they walked, the almost imperceptible pull between them that made her heart quicken with every passing breath.

But something more lingered—something darker and more dangerous. The fragments of memories, flashes that came and went like lightning strikes, leaving behind only the faintest afterimage. Faces she couldn't place, voices that echoed in the quiet spaces of her mind. The lingering sensation of soft lips, the warmth of arms around her—but it was always just out of reach, fading like a half-remembered dream.

"I can feel it too," Elyndra's voice broke through the silence, soft yet heavy with the weight of something she hadn't said. "The pull. The memories—they're coming back."

Veyrina glanced at her, the strange connection between them flickering in the air. "I don't understand," she whispered, her voice barely audible against the wind that began to stir through the ancient stones. "Why now? Why are these memories resurfacing?"

Elyndra's expression darkened for a moment, as if the answer pained her. "The realm calls to us. It knows we've forgotten… but we must remember. Everything hinges on it."

Veyrina felt a shiver run down her spine. The atmosphere around them seemed to thicken, pressing in on her chest, as if the very air was heavy with the weight of unspoken truths. And yet, there was also an undeniable pull—one that tugged at her heart and made her want to reach out, to ask the questions that danced on the edge of her mind.

But she hesitated. There was something there—something in Elyndra's eyes, something she couldn't quite trust. Was it a shared history that had bound them together? Or was there something darker, more complicated, buried between them? Her heart clenched as an overwhelming sense of unease washed over her.

The echoes of the past grew louder, a soft hum in the background of her thoughts, a constant presence that never fully faded. The wind picked up, its wail now sounding like a distant, mournful cry. The air seemed to shimmer, and Veyrina's pulse quickened as the landscape around them began to shift.

A clearing opened before them, bathed in an eerie glow. The light was unnatural, cast by nothing visible, but the very stones of the ground beneath their feet seemed to pulse with an otherworldly energy, drawing them forward. A set of ancient ruins loomed in the distance—its silhouette dark against the dimming sky.

Without a word, Elyndra began walking toward it, and Veyrina followed, drawn by an invisible force she couldn't name. They crossed the threshold of the ruin, entering a place where the air seemed even colder, sharper. The walls were etched with strange symbols, their meanings lost to time, but the shapes were familiar—circles within circles, spirals intertwining with jagged lines. They were a language of the old world, a language that tugged at the very core of Veyrina's being.

"Do you know what this is?" Veyrina asked, her voice strained.

Elyndra nodded, her gaze fixed on the carvings. "These are the markings of our past. A reminder of what we once were—of what we lost."

Veyrina stepped closer to the wall, her fingers brushing the stone as she traced the patterns. The moment her skin made contact, a jolt of energy shot through her, and the world seemed to lurch. Her vision blurred for an instant, and she gasped as the memories rushed in like a tide—unbidden and uncontrollable.

She was standing in a different place, in a different time. She could feel the warmth of the sun on her skin, the scent of flowers in the air. Elyndra was beside her, her smile bright and full of promise. Their hands were intertwined, fingers brushing against each other in a familiar gesture that made her heart ache.

But just as quickly, the vision flickered, and Veyrina was back in the ruins, her chest heaving as she struggled to breathe. The overwhelming feeling of love—the connection—was still there, lingering, like a thread tied around her heart.

Elyndra was staring at her, her eyes filled with something unreadable. "Do you remember now?" she asked, her voice barely above a whisper.

"I…" Veyrina shook her head, her breath coming in ragged gasps. "I don't know. It's all so… fragmented. So broken."

The air seemed to grow heavier, pressing in on her chest. Veyrina's mind was reeling from the fragments of memories that swirled in her mind, jumbled and incomplete. She had seen herself with Elyndra, in a moment of tenderness, but she couldn't hold onto it. It slipped through her fingers like water, leaving nothing but the taste of longing.

Elyndra took a step toward her, her eyes softening. "It's all right," she said, her voice steady, but there was a flicker of something darker behind her words. "We will remember. Together."

But Veyrina couldn't shake the feeling that something was wrong. The words didn't sit right with her. Elyndra was too calm, too composed, as if she already knew what was happening—what they were about to face.

"I don't know if I can trust you," Veyrina said before she could stop herself. The words hung in the air between them, a crack that widened with each passing second. She could feel the tension building, like the quiet before a storm.

Elyndra's expression faltered for the briefest moment, but it was enough for Veyrina to notice. She opened her mouth to speak, but the sound of something scraping against the stone interrupted her.

Veyrina's heart leaped in her chest as she turned to face the source of the sound. A figure emerged from the shadows, tall and cloaked in darkness. His presence was unmistakable—unnatural. The figure's eyes gleamed with an eerie light, and the air around him seemed to shift, swirling like the tendrils of smoke.

"You've come," the figure's voice was a low, menacing rumble. "The key is within your grasp. But you will not find it so easily."

Veyrina's instincts screamed at her to run, to escape, but her feet were frozen in place. She couldn't take her eyes off the figure, whose every movement seemed to bend the very fabric of the realm around them.

Elyndra stepped in front of Veyrina, her posture tense, defensive. "Who are you?" she demanded, her voice sharp, but there was an underlying tremor to it that betrayed her fear.

The figure tilted his head, his smile wide and full of malice. "I am the one who guards the truth. The one who will decide whether or not you are worthy of the knowledge you seek."

Veyrina's pulse quickened as the figure's gaze shifted to her, cold and calculating. "You," he said, his voice lowering to a dangerous whisper. "You are the key. The one who holds the last piece of the puzzle."

The world seemed to close in on Veyrina as the weight of his words sank in. She had felt the pull of something, but she hadn't realized it was her own destiny that had brought her here.

The figure took a step forward, and the ground beneath

them rumbled. "But the price will be high, little one. Are you prepared to pay it?"

A chilling silence followed, broken only by the echoes that now seemed to grow louder, drowning out everything else. The past, the present, and the future—all of it was converging in this moment. And Veyrina realized, with a sinking feeling, that there was no turning back.

Her mind raced, but one thought remained at the forefront—she was about to face a truth that would change everything.

The figure's gaze didn't leave Veyrina. It was like he was seeing straight into her soul, his piercing eyes stripping away all pretense. She could feel the weight of his scrutiny pressing on her chest, as if he were weighing her very existence. Her heart raced, blood pounding in her ears.

"I—I don't understand," Veyrina stammered, her voice barely above a whisper. The air around them felt thick, almost suffocating, as if the very atmosphere was alive with the tension between them.

The figure didn't answer right away. Instead, he raised a hand, slowly, as if savoring the moment, then gestured toward the dark, swirling energy around them. "You were never meant to forget, child of time," he said, his voice smooth but layered with menace. "The echoes of your past were sealed, but you have opened them. And now… the price must be paid."

Elyndra moved closer to Veyrina, a protective stance that spoke volumes of her hidden fears. "We're not here for games, shadow," she said, her voice filled with authority. "We want the truth. What is this place? What is the key you speak of?"

The figure's laugh was soft at first, then grew louder, reverberating through the stone walls, echoing unnervingly in the chamber. "The truth," he mused, his eyes flickering with amusement. "The truth is a powerful thing, isn't it? It can tear apart the strongest of bonds, break even the most sacred of promises. But you, Elyndra Varell, you should know that by now."

Veyrina's heart skipped. She turned her head toward Elyndra, searching her face for some hint, some clue to the mystery. But Elyndra's face remained unreadable, her jaw tight.

"What do you know about her?" Veyrina demanded, her voice trembling, but her resolve hardening. "What is it that you're not telling me?"

The figure took a step forward, a long, slow stride that seemed to cause the shadows to stretch and writhe at his feet. "Ah, so the amnesia is still intact," he said, almost to himself, his smile widening. "You do not remember, do you? You do not remember the love you and Elyndra once shared, the bond forged in the deepest recesses of time itself."

Veyrina blinked, her pulse thundering in her ears. Elyndra's silence spoke volumes, and a new wave of unease began to coil in her stomach. Could it be true? Were they connected in some way, beyond the shadows of this realm? But she couldn't remember. She couldn't remember anything past the present moment, and yet, something inside her pulled at her to trust Elyndra, to believe in her despite the growing uncertainties.

"Stop playing games!" Veyrina snapped, stepping forward. "Tell me what's going on. Who are you, really? Why are we here?"

The figure's smile faltered, and for the briefest of moments, his eyes darkened with a fury that made the ground beneath them tremble. But just as quickly, he regained his composure. "I am the Guardian of the Echo, the keeper of all forgotten truths. And you, Veyrina Lioris, are part of a much larger design. A design you have yet to comprehend."

Elyndra stepped forward then, her eyes narrowing, her hand instinctively reaching for the hilt of her dagger, though the motion seemed more out of habit than genuine threat. "You speak in riddles," she said coldly, "but your words carry too much weight. What exactly are you saying? Why have you called us here?"

The figure tilted his head, considering her question. "Ah, the noble one," he murmured. "You were always the skeptic, the one who doubted, even when the evidence was in front of you. But you, too, have a part to play in this. You both do."

A tense silence filled the room, thick and suffocating. Then, as if everything had been building to this single moment, the figure's smile grew wide and feral.

"The Echo will reveal the truth," he said softly. "And when it does, you will both remember… everything."

Before either of them could respond, the air around them seemed to snap, and the ground trembled with a sudden force. Veyrina gasped, stumbling back as the stone beneath her feet cracked open, revealing a glowing fissure that pulsed with an eerie light. A cold wind swept through the room, carrying with it the sound of distant voices—whispers in an unknown tongue. The wind seemed to push them toward the fissure, the pull irresistible.

"No," Elyndra shouted, reaching out to grab Veyrina's arm. "We don't have to follow this! We can—"

But before she could finish, the wind grew stronger, and Veyrina felt herself being tugged forward, her feet dragging against the stone floor as the fissure grew wider. The air around them buzzed with electricity, and the whispers grew louder, a cacophony of voices that filled the very air. Veyrina could hear her name being called, over and over again, from every direction, as if her very soul was being summoned.

And then, the figure—the Guardian of the Echo—spoke again, his voice echoing in the midst of the chaos. "You will find what you seek within the Echo, Veyrina. But beware, for the truth is not always a gift. Sometimes it is a curse."

As Veyrina struggled against the pull, Elyndra tightened her grip, trying desperately to hold her back. "We can't go in there! The Echo is not what you think it is. It will only show you parts of the past you're not ready to see!"

But the more Veyrina fought against it, the stronger the pull became. The fissure widened even more, the blinding light within it intensifying until it consumed her vision completely. She could hear Elyndra's voice, but it sounded so far away, as if she were being drawn into a different world.

Finally, Veyrina's feet slipped from beneath her, and she was pulled into the glowing chasm. A surge of light and power enveloped her, blinding her completely, and for a moment, she felt as though she were falling through an endless void.

And then, with a sudden, violent jolt, she landed on solid ground.

When Veyrina opened her eyes, she was no longer in the ruins. She was standing in a vast, impossibly dark landscape, the sky above her swirling with clouds of dark, shifting shadows. A cold mist clung to the ground, and in the distance, she could make out a silhouette of something large—an enormous structure, ancient and broken, rising from the earth like a monument to something long forgotten.

The Echo.

The realization hit her all at once.

She had been pulled into the very heart of the Echo, the place where time itself twisted and fragmented. The place where her past, and her future, were now intertwined.

And standing beside her, as if she had always been there, was Elyndra.

"Welcome," Elyndra's voice came from beside her, softer now, almost wistful. "To the place where we lost everything. And the place where we may find it all again."

Veyrina turned to her, her heart pounding. "What is this place?" she asked, her voice barely a whisper.

Elyndra's expression darkened, her gaze fixed on the horizon where the broken structure loomed. "The Echo," she said. "The place where all lost things come to rest… and where the truth waits to be revealed."

Three

The Heart of the Echo

The air in the temple was thick, humid with the scent of moss and old stone, each breath carrying the taste of something long forgotten. The dim light from the fissure they had entered cast eerie shadows across the crumbling walls, the once-pristine architecture now a ruin of its former grandeur. Strange symbols were etched into the stone, curling in patterns Veyrina couldn't quite comprehend, but they seemed to pulse with a faint, rhythmical energy, as if the temple itself were alive.

Veyrina's fingers brushed the cool, smooth surface of the ancient column they passed, the texture sending a shiver up her spine. It was unlike anything she had ever seen, and yet… it felt so familiar. Like she had walked these halls before, under a different sky, a different time.

At her side, Elyndra moved with a quiet intensity, her gaze darting back and forth, as if anticipating danger. The tension between them had settled into an uneasy silence, the pull of their connection drawing them closer even as their memories remained fractured. They were both searching for something— a truth that remained just out of reach.

As they ventured deeper into the temple, the atmosphere grew heavier, the air crackling with an unseen power. It was as if the walls themselves were watching them, waiting for them to unravel the mystery.

Veyrina's heart beat faster as they approached a raised dais at the center of the chamber. Atop it rested an orb—its surface shimmering with an ethereal light, so beautiful that it nearly took her breath away. It was unlike anything she had seen before, a perfect sphere of translucent crystal, its interior swirling with iridescent colors that shifted and danced like the very essence of the stars.

"This is it," Elyndra murmured, her voice barely audible, as if the air itself was too thick to carry sound. She stepped forward, her hand reaching toward the orb. "This is the key. I can feel it."

Veyrina hesitated, a strange mixture of curiosity and apprehension flooding her chest. Her fingers tingled, urging her forward, but something deep inside whispered that this moment, this choice, was more than just a simple action. The orb, pulsing with energy, seemed to call to her, beckoning her to come closer.

"Are you sure?" Veyrina asked, her voice low, uncertain.

Elyndra turned to her, eyes filled with a mixture of fear and resolve. "We don't have a choice. The Echo brought us here for a reason. This... this is where everything begins." She glanced back at the orb, her fingers brushing the air above it. "It's waiting for us."

Despite her trepidation, Veyrina stepped up beside her. The air felt charged, heavy with the promise of something ancient, something powerful. Without another word, Elyndra's hand hovered over the orb, and Veyrina's heart skipped a beat as she placed her own hand beside it.

As their fingers made contact, a shock of energy coursed through their bodies. The world around them seemed to shudder, the temple groaning as if waking from a deep slumber. The orb flared with brilliant light, and for a brief, dizzying moment, Veyrina felt as if she were falling through time itself, her body weightless and suspended in an endless abyss.

Then, as quickly as it began, the sensation stopped.

Veyrina gasped, her hand pulling away from the orb as if burned, but Elyndra's grip remained firm. Her eyes were wide, filled with an emotion Veyrina couldn't quite place. She turned to Veyrina, lips parted as if to speak, but before either of them could make a sound, the entire temple began to tremble.

The ground beneath their feet cracked with a deafening roar, and a blast of energy sent them both stumbling backward. Stone columns shattered, falling with a crash as the walls shook violently. Veyrina's heart raced as she gripped Elyndra's arm, both of them scrambling to keep their balance amid the chaos.

"We need to get out of here!" Veyrina shouted, her voice drowned out by the thunderous noise of the collapsing temple. The ceiling above them cracked, large chunks of rock tumbling down. She could feel the heat radiating from the orb, its energy now a dangerous force that was tearing the temple apart.

Elyndra nodded, her face pale, but her eyes were fixed on the orb. "It's the Echo," she said through gritted teeth. "It's awakening… and it's angry."

Suddenly, a deafening roar echoed through the temple, a

deep, guttural sound that seemed to reverberate in their very bones. From the shadows at the far end of the chamber, something moved—fast, predatory, and unmistakably alive. Veyrina's pulse spiked in fear as a figure emerged from the darkness.

The creature that stepped into the flickering light was humanoid, but twisted—its form shifting like smoke, the edges of its body jagged and uneven. Its face was obscured by a hood, but two glowing eyes, an unnatural shade of gold, gleamed beneath the shadows. It was a being of the Echo—a guardian of sorts, Veyrina realized, the very force that had awoken with the relic's activation.

It took a slow, deliberate step toward them, and the air grew colder, the temperature plummeting. The creature's presence felt suffocating, as if the very space around them was being drawn into its vortex.

"Leave," the creature rasped, its voice low and rumbling. "The Echo does not suffer trespassers. Your meddling has sealed your fate."

Veyrina stood frozen, her heart hammering against her ribcage. The being's eyes locked onto hers, and for a brief moment, she could have sworn she saw something familiar— something in the depth of those golden orbs that stirred a memory deep within her. A flicker of recognition, something just beyond her grasp.

"You… you know us," she whispered, the words slipping from her lips before she could stop them. The realization hit her like a wave. The connection between them wasn't just an abstract force—it was personal.

The creature's lips curled into a cruel smile, and it took another step forward, its presence swallowing the light around them. "Yes," it said, its voice echoing through the temple. "You were once mine. And now, you will return to the place you belong."

Before Veyrina could respond, Elyndra stepped in front of her, her body a shield. "No," she snapped, voice sharp. "We don't belong to you. We're not here to submit—we're here to learn the truth."

The creature's eyes flickered with a hint of amusement. "The truth?" it echoed, its voice dripping with disdain. "You think you can change the course of fate? The truth you seek is buried deep within the Echo, and only the Echo itself can decide if you're worthy to know it."

With a sudden, terrifying motion, the creature raised one hand, and a wave of dark energy surged toward them. Veyrina barely had time to react as Elyndra threw herself in front of her, the energy crashing against her shield with a force that knocked them both to the ground. The shockwave sent the temple into a final, chaotic collapse.

"Elyndra!" Veyrina screamed, scrambling to her feet. She reached out, her hand catching Elyndra's as the rubble continued to fall around them. "We need to go!"

But Elyndra's eyes were focused, unblinking. She stood, gritting her teeth against the force of the collapsing temple. "We can't leave yet. The key is here. We need it to understand what's happened."

The guardian stepped forward, its movements unnaturally graceful for its monstrous form. "You cannot stop the Echo. It will consume you. It has already consumed your past, and now it will consume your future."

With a final burst of energy, the guardian launched itself toward them, a tendril of dark power trailing behind it.

Veyrina and Elyndra barely managed to dodge as the creature struck, sending debris flying in all directions. Veyrina's heart was in her throat, but she didn't hesitate. She grabbed Elyndra's hand tightly, pulling her toward the heart of the temple, where the orb pulsed with an undeniable power.

"The orb," Veyrina gasped. "We need to destroy it!"

But as her fingers brushed against it again, the pulse grew stronger, the very air vibrating with raw, untamed magic.

The Echo was alive, and it would not let them go so easily.

The tension in the air was suffocating, the very walls of the ancient temple trembling with the power that emanated from the orb. Veyrina's hand still gripped Elyndra's, but her fingers trembled as they reached toward the glowing sphere. She could feel the overwhelming pull of its energy, a force as ancient as time itself, thrumming beneath her skin, calling out to something deep within her soul.

"Elyndra…" Veyrina whispered, her voice shaky. "If we don't destroy it, the Echo will consume us—our memories, our very existence. We can't let it win."

But Elyndra's eyes, wide with a mixture of fear and determination, did not leave the orb. Her grip tightened around Veyrina's hand, and her voice was steady, but there was an underlying urgency. "No. We can't destroy it. It's the key. We have to understand it. The answers we've been searching for are inside."

Veyrina's heart pounded in her chest. The very walls around them felt alive, alive with an ancient and powerful energy that threatened to crush them. The temple was collapsing around them, the ceiling shuddering as pieces of stone broke away, crashing to the ground with thunderous sounds.

But Veyrina couldn't look away from Elyndra's gaze. She saw the desperation in her eyes, the same desperation that matched her own.

"I don't trust it," Veyrina whispered, pulling Elyndra closer to her. The guardian, a twisted creature of shadow, loomed in the background, its eyes gleaming with malice. "I don't trust any of this."

Elyndra's face softened for a brief moment. She let go of Veyrina's hand, stepping forward towards the orb, her eyes filled with something Veyrina couldn't quite place. "We've been lost in the Echo for so long. But we can't be afraid of it anymore. This is our destiny, Veyrina. This is how we'll uncover who we were, who we are meant to be."

For a moment, everything else faded into the background. The collapsing temple, the howling winds, the dark shadows chasing them—it all disappeared in the wake of Elyndra's conviction. It was as if her words had become the only truth left in the world.

Veyrina swallowed hard, her gaze shifting to the orb. The intensity of the connection between them made her pulse race, made her chest ache with longing. A familiar warmth swirled inside her, the pull of their bond undeniable. She knew, without a doubt, that Elyndra was right. The answers they sought—answers that could unlock their past, could reveal the truth of their love—were within their reach.

Before she could speak, a deafening roar echoed from the depths of the collapsing temple, and the guardian surged forward, its massive form blocking their path to the orb. The creature's golden eyes locked onto theirs with an intensity that made Veyrina's breath catch in her throat.

"You think you can control it?" The guardian's voice was low, a gravelly hiss that seemed to come from everywhere at once. "You cannot. The Echo was never meant for you."

Veyrina took a step back, instinctively pulling Elyndra away. The creature was advancing, its form shifting, warping like smoke. The very air seemed to grow thicker, the temperature plummeting as the guardian's power pulsed with a malevolent force.

Elyndra didn't move. Her eyes were locked on the orb, her face a mask of determination. "We have to face it. We can't let it stop us."

Veyrina hesitated for a moment. Her entire being screamed for them to run, to escape this nightmare before it consumed them. But deep down, she knew Elyndra was right. There was no turning back. Not now.

"We'll face it together," Veyrina said, her voice stronger now, steady with resolve. "We're in this together."

The guardian's laugh echoed through the crumbling temple, dark and foreboding. "Together? You have no idea what you are truly up against. The Echo is far more powerful than you know."

Without warning, the guardian lunged at them, a blur of shadow, its hand outstretched to strike. Veyrina gasped, pulling Elyndra toward her, but the guardian was too fast. In one fluid motion, it lashed out, sending a powerful shockwave that threw them both to the ground.

The force of the blow left Veyrina gasping for air, her head spinning. Elyndra cried out beside her, the sound of it sharp and desperate. The temple's walls seemed to collapse faster now, as if the very structure was collapsing under the weight of the conflict, the Echo's power growing stronger by the second.

"Elyndra!" Veyrina shouted, scrambling to her feet. She reached for Elyndra, pulling her into her arms. "We have to fight back. We can't let it tear us apart."

The guardian loomed over them, its eyes blazing with fury. It opened its mouth wide, and for a moment, Veyrina thought she could hear a low, mournful song—a faint, haunting echo that seemed to resonate in her very bones. It was a melody she recognized, one she couldn't place, but it filled her with a deep sorrow, as if she had once heard it before.

"Do you hear it?" Elyndra whispered, her voice shaking as she held onto Veyrina. "The song… the Echo. It's calling us."

Veyrina's heart pounded, her pulse racing in her ears as she stared at the orb. The light from it flickered, its energy pulsing, brighter now, as if it had a life of its own. It was as though the very essence of their connection—their love—was tied to the Echo, tied to the temple's ruinous power.

The guardian took a step forward, its form shifting and growing darker, more monstrous. "You cannot fight fate. You cannot fight the Echo. It is eternal."

Elyndra's voice was fierce, her grip on Veyrina tightening. "We don't need to fight it. We need to understand it."

Veyrina felt the pull again, stronger this time. The echo, the connection, the love that had once bound them together—it was all coming back. A flood of emotions surged through her: longing, pain, betrayal, but also an overwhelming sense of purpose.

She stood, pulling Elyndra with her. Their hands clasped tightly together. They couldn't let the Echo consume them— not again. Not after all they had lost.

As the guardian raised its hand to strike once more, Veyrina closed her eyes, feeling the energy within the orb. She could feel it—a surge of power, an awakening. This was the moment. The key.

In one swift motion, Veyrina thrust her hand toward the orb, pulling Elyndra with her. The energy coursed through her body, radiating from the orb and into her very soul. It was like nothing she had ever experienced before. It was ancient and boundless, an overwhelming force of connection and understanding.

The temple trembled again, but this time, it was not the force of the collapsing walls that made it shake. It was the power of their bond—their love—that resonated through the temple, shaking it to its foundations.

The guardian howled in fury, but it was no longer in control. The orb's light grew blinding, and the echoes of the past came rushing back, memories flooding Veyrina's mind, flooding Elyndra's as well.

She saw it then—visions of them, together, long ago. Of their love, fierce and pure, a love that had been torn apart by forces they didn't understand. And the echoes… they were not just of their past—they were their future too.

With a final, resounding crack, the orb shattered, its light engulfing the temple.

Veyrina and Elyndra collapsed to their knees as the energy exploded, the walls collapsing inwards around them, the guardian's form dissolving into the ether.

And in that moment, the Echo was silent.

The temple fell silent. Time itself seemed to still.

But the future—**their future**—was now in their hands.

Four

Bonds of Light and Shadow

The air was heavy as Veyrina and Elyndra stepped away from the temple ruins, their bodies bruised, their minds still reeling from the surge of energy that had consumed them. It felt as though they had broken through some barrier, but at the same time, they had only just begun to unravel the enigma that bound them together.

The land surrounding them had changed. The temple, once hidden in the heart of a dense forest, now seemed like an isolated relic standing in the middle of an unending wasteland, the sky above split into an unnatural blend of light and shadow. On one side, the horizon was bathed in a soft, golden glow, the remnants of the sun casting long shadows across the cracked earth. On the other side, dark clouds swirled, churning with an unnatural energy, their dark tendrils creeping ever closer.

Elyndra stood at the edge of the rift, her fingers brushing the air, as if trying to catch the wisps of shadow that darted in and out of the light. Her face was taut, her lips pressed together in a line of concentration. Veyrina could feel the tension radiating from her, like a tightly wound coil, ready to snap.

"Elyndra," Veyrina murmured, stepping closer. "What is this place?"

Elyndra didn't respond right away. She seemed lost in thought, her eyes drawn to the swirling rift that divided the sky. The glow of the light seemed to reach for her, as if beckoning her, but the shadow refused to release its grip.

"It's the rift," Elyndra said finally, her voice strained, low. "The place where our pasts meet. The divide between light and shadow. I thought… I thought it was a myth."

Veyrina frowned. "A myth?"

Elyndra turned to her, her expression conflicted, like someone caught between two worlds. "I thought it was a legend. But now… now it feels real. This place… it feels like home, but also… like a prison."

Veyrina stepped closer, her gaze following the line where the rift split the sky. There was something about it, something familiar, as though she had seen it before, but in a dream. A sense of deja vu washed over her, a sensation that made her skin crawl.

"Is this where we were separated?" Veyrina asked, her voice almost a whisper. "Where we lost everything?"

Elyndra's eyes hardened, and her shoulders tensed, a subtle shift in her stance that Veyrina didn't miss. For a moment, she thought Elyndra might say something, but instead, Elyndra simply nodded, the movement slow and deliberate.

Before Veyrina could speak again, a shadow flickered in the corner of her vision—a dark figure, moving swiftly across the land.

Veyrina's hand instinctively reached for the dagger at her side, her body coiling with readiness. But before she could make a move, the figure emerged from the shadows, stepping into the fading light.

A man.

He was tall, with long dark hair that whipped in the wind, his eyes a piercing shade of violet. His features were sharp, regal almost, but there was a dark edge to him, something that made Veyrina instinctively tense, even as the figure came to a halt before them.

Elyndra's breath hitched, a sharp intake of air that did not go unnoticed by Veyrina. She could feel the shift in the air, the sudden tension that crackled between the two women.

"I see you've found her," the man said, his voice rich, low, and full of a strange familiarity.

Veyrina's gaze flickered between Elyndra and the stranger, confusion growing in her chest. Elyndra took a slow step backward, her body stiff, as if she were trying to retreat from something she had not yet fully accepted.

"Xyrian," Elyndra finally spoke, her voice strained, hesitant. "What are you doing here?"

Veyrina's brow furrowed. "Who is this?"

Xyrian's lips twisted into a smile that didn't reach his eyes. "You don't remember me, do you, Elyndra?" He stepped closer, his movements deliberate, like a predator circling its prey. "Funny, I remember you."

Elyndra's face hardened, and Veyrina could see the conflict in her eyes, the way her fists clenched at her sides. The air around them shifted, growing colder as Xyrian's presence seemed to stir something deep within Elyndra.

"This is Xyrian," Elyndra said, her voice cold now. "My… my

former lover."

Veyrina's stomach churned at the words. The implications hung in the air, unspoken but heavy, like a dark cloud. For a moment, she said nothing, her mind racing with a thousand thoughts she could not process.

Xyrian's gaze turned to Veyrina, his eyes narrowing slightly. "You must be the one who's supposed to be her salvation," he said, his voice dripping with sarcasm. "I hope you know what you're getting into."

Veyrina's grip tightened on her dagger, but Elyndra's hand shot out to stop her, her touch gentle but firm.

"Don't," Elyndra said quietly, her eyes never leaving Xyrian's face. "He's not our enemy."

Veyrina's heart pounded in her chest. "How can you say that? He's—"

"I know," Elyndra interrupted, her tone sharp. "I know what he is. But I also know that he's part of my past, and we can't escape that. We can't escape the choices that brought us here."

Xyrian's smile widened, but there was no warmth in it. "Ah, but you're forgetting, aren't you, Elyndra? You think you can just ignore your past, pretend it doesn't matter. But it does. It always has."

Veyrina's pulse quickened. "What are you talking about?"

Xyrian's gaze turned back to her, his expression shifting slightly, as if a memory had flickered behind his eyes. "You don't even know, do you?" he asked softly. "You don't know what really happened between us. Between all of us."

Elyndra's jaw clenched. "Enough, Xyrian. We don't have time for this. We need to understand what's happening here, not dredge up old ghosts."

Xyrian's eyes flicked to the rift above them, the dark clouds swirling as if in response to his words. "The rift," he said softly, almost to himself. "It's where everything began. Where it all went wrong."

Veyrina turned her gaze to the rift, a sense of foreboding sweeping over her. Something about the rift, about the way Xyrian spoke of it, made her feel as though they were standing on the edge of something far darker than they had yet realized.

"We have to go," Elyndra said, pulling Veyrina's attention back to her. "Now."

Xyrian's laughter followed them as they turned to leave, the sound lingering in the air like a curse.

"You'll regret this," he called after them. "You'll see. The light and the shadow, they always find a way to consume you."

Veyrina couldn't shake the feeling that something had shifted between them, that this encounter with Xyrian—this ghost from Elyndra's past—was just the beginning. She could feel the weight of the rift pressing on her, the darkness creeping closer with every step they took.

And as they ventured deeper into the heart of the shadow realm, Veyrina realized that their love—whatever it was, whatever it had been—was no longer enough to protect them from the forces that sought to tear them apart.

Something far greater was at play. And they were running out of time.

The tension between them had only grown since their encounter with Xyrian. Elyndra's shoulders remained tense, her steps measured as if each one carried the weight of a memory she had not yet reconciled. Veyrina couldn't help but watch her closely, her gaze lingering on the way Elyndra's fingers would twitch at her side, as if resisting some invisible pull.

The air felt different now, oppressive in a way that pressed against Veyrina's chest with each breath. The rift loomed above them, a dark scar in the sky that seemed to pulse with an otherworldly energy. The shadows twisted and writhed, reacting to every movement, every word spoken.

"Where are we going?" Veyrina finally asked, her voice breaking the silence between them. They had been walking for what felt like hours, though the sun never seemed to move, caught in the stasis of the rift.

Elyndra didn't answer right away. She seemed lost in thought, her expression distant, as if her mind were elsewhere. When she finally spoke, her voice was barely above a whisper. "I don't know," she said, her eyes flicking nervously to the dark horizon. "I'm not sure where we're supposed to go. The rift… it changes. It's not just a place—it's a state of being. It pulls you in, twists your thoughts."

Veyrina could feel the weight of her words. There was something almost tangible in the way Elyndra spoke, something raw and unspoken. Veyrina's heart twisted in her chest, a mixture of sympathy and frustration bubbling within her. She wanted to help, to reach the heart of this, but Elyndra seemed so locked in her past, so bound by the shadows that clung to her.

And then, as if on cue, the wind shifted. The once-calm air grew heavy, thick with the scent of ozone and decay. A dark shape moved against the horizon—something that hadn't been there before, something that seemed to form out of the very shadows themselves. Veyrina instinctively stepped closer to Elyndra, her eyes scanning the movement in the distance.

The shape drew closer, and Veyrina's breath caught in her throat.

It was a creature of darkness, its form shifting and writhing like smoke, its eyes burning with a fierce, violet light. It moved with unsettling speed, its jagged limbs extending and retracting with every step, as though the creature itself were part of the rift—something born from its depths.

"Elyndra," Veyrina said, her voice taut with warning. "What is that?"

Elyndra's eyes widened, her face paling as she instinctively took a step back. "A guardian," she said, her voice trembling. "One of the sentinels of the rift."

Veyrina's pulse quickened. "A sentinel? What does it want?"

Elyndra swallowed, her eyes flickering between the approaching figure and Veyrina. "It doesn't want anything. It's here to stop us from leaving."

The creature moved closer, its form shifting more rapidly now, as though it were growing agitated. Veyrina instinctively reached for her dagger, but Elyndra's hand shot out, stopping her.

"Don't," Elyndra warned, her grip tight on Veyrina's wrist. "It's not here to kill us—not yet. But if we don't pass the trial, it will. We have to face it."

Veyrina's brow furrowed. "Trial?"

"Yes," Elyndra replied, her voice soft but firm. "The rift… it's not just a place. It's a test. A test of what we are willing to sacrifice, of what we can face within ourselves."

The creature reached the edge of their path, its form now fully materialized—a towering, ethereal being with shimmering, translucent skin and dark veins running beneath it, like cracks in a shattered mirror. Its eyes gleamed with an intelligence that made Veyrina's stomach churn.

Without a word, the creature raised a hand, its fingers splaying outwards as if preparing to strike.

Elyndra stepped forward, drawing in a steadying breath. "We must face our past," she murmured. "That's the trial. It will show us what we fear most."

Veyrina's heart skipped a beat. She wasn't sure what was happening, but her instinct screamed at her to prepare for something she wasn't ready for.

The creature's eyes locked on Elyndra, and with a sharp gesture, it sent a pulse of dark energy toward them. Veyrina barely had time to react before the force hit her—throwing her backwards into the dirt, her body slamming into the ground with a painful thud. She gasped for breath, feeling the weight of the rift pressing in around her, as though the very air were suffocating her.

Elyndra cried out, falling to her knees beside Veyrina, her hands trembling as she reached out to help her. "Veyrina! Are you okay?"

"I'm… I'm fine," Veyrina managed to say, though her head was spinning. Her hands clenched the ground, grounding herself against the intensity of the pulse. The pain was still sharp, but there was something else, too—an overwhelming sense of dread that flooded her mind, as if her very soul were being tested.

The creature's form wavered, its eyes narrowing in concentration as it studied them.

"Face it," Elyndra urged, her voice strained but determined. "Face your greatest fear. It's the only way we can move forward."

Veyrina swallowed, her heart thundering in her chest. She wasn't sure what that meant, but she knew that they had no choice but to try. She had to confront whatever it was that had been buried deep within her.

Suddenly, the ground beneath them trembled, and the air seemed to distort, like a mirage. Images began to flood Veyrina's mind—fractured, blurry memories that didn't feel like her own. Flashbacks of people she didn't recognize, moments of warmth and pain, loss and grief. Faces she couldn't place, voices she couldn't remember.

Then, the images began to focus—sharp and clear. She was standing in a room, a cold stone chamber lit by flickering candlelight. A figure stood before her, a woman, her face obscured by shadows. The woman's hand reached out, fingers trembling, but Veyrina couldn't move. Her body was frozen, as if trapped in time.

"No," Veyrina whispered, her voice shaking. "No, this can't be real."

But the vision continued. The woman's hand grew closer, the touch of her fingers soft but cold as ice. And then, suddenly, a name slipped from the woman's lips—her voice low and haunting.

"Veyrina."

Veyrina's heart seemed to stop in her chest. The woman's face began to emerge from the shadows, revealing a face that sent a shudder through her very soul.

It was Elyndra.

The world around her seemed to spin, the vision fading and shifting as the rift pulled at her. She could feel the echo of the past crashing through her, the fragments of memories blending together in a haze of fear and longing.

Elyndra's voice called out to her, snapping Veyrina back to the present. "Veyrina!"

Veyrina gasped, her eyes widening as she came back to herself. The creature was still there, watching them intently, its violet eyes gleaming with dark amusement.

"I don't know what this is," Veyrina said, her voice trembling with emotion, her body still numb from the strange vision. "But I don't want to lose you again."

Elyndra reached for her, her hand gentle but firm. "You won't," she said softly. "We have to face it. We have to face what we are."

The creature raised its hand once more, and a deep rumble filled the air, but this time, it was not an attack. The trial was not about defeating an enemy—it was about conquering what lay within.

Veyrina took a deep breath, her hand finding Elyndra's, and together, they faced the creature and the rift—the shadows that had defined them for so long.

The trial had only just begun. And the darkness they were about to confront was far deeper than either of them could have imagined.

Five

The Depths of Desire

The air grew thicker with every step they took, charged with a strange, almost tangible energy. It was as though the very fabric of the realm was attuned to their movements, responding to the pull of the echo that bound them. Veyrina could feel it—a gnawing sensation deep in her chest, a hunger she couldn't quite understand. It was a longing, a need, that intensified the closer she got to Elyndra.

Their journey through the realm had taken them deeper into the heart of its mysteries, and with each passing hour, Veyrina could sense the growing weight of their shared connection. It was more than just the echo—they were bound by something older, more primal, something that reverberated through the very core of her being.

Elyndra walked beside her, her presence both comforting and unsettling. The tension between them was palpable, like the flickering of a flame in the dark, its heat both inviting and dangerous. Veyrina could see it in Elyndra's eyes, the same longing, the same fear. Neither of them had spoken of it openly, but it hung between them like an unspoken truth.

"I don't know how much longer I can fight it," Veyrina whispered, her voice low and laden with a mixture of frustration and longing.

Elyndra didn't respond at first, her gaze fixed ahead, her lips pressed into a thin line. She, too, was struggling with the pull—there was no mistaking that. But for her, it was different. The walls she had built around her emotions were breaking down, and she didn't know if she was ready to face the consequences of what that would mean.

"You're not the only one," Elyndra finally replied, her voice strained. "But I can't… I can't give in to it. Not yet. We don't know what it will cost us."

Veyrina stopped in her tracks, her hand instinctively reaching for Elyndra's arm. "And if the cost is our happiness? Or our hearts? What if that's what we're meant to find here?"

Elyndra turned to face her, her expression tense, but there was a flicker of something softer beneath the surface—something that mirrored the storm inside Veyrina. For a moment, the world seemed to pause, the air still and heavy with unspoken words.

"I'm afraid," Elyndra admitted quietly, her voice barely above a whisper. "Afraid of what it means. Afraid of what we might become."

Veyrina's heart clenched, her pulse quickening. She wanted to reach out, to take Elyndra's hand and pull her close, but something—some invisible force—held her back. She knew the dangers of what lay ahead, and yet, the pull of Elyndra's presence was undeniable.

"Don't be afraid," Veyrina whispered, her voice thick with emotion. "We're not alone. We have each other."

Elyndra's eyes softened, but there was still a shadow behind them, a wariness that refused to fade. She glanced away, her gaze drifting toward the horizon where the realm's shifting landscape seemed to stretch on forever. "I wish that were enough."

Veyrina's hand dropped slowly to her side, and the weight of the moment settled between them. There was a chasm between them now—an invisible line that neither dared to cross. And yet, Veyrina couldn't help but feel the pull of something more, something she couldn't explain. The echoes whispered to her, urging her forward, urging her to embrace what was coming.

Suddenly, the ground beneath them trembled. A low rumble reverberated through the earth, sending a shiver of unease through Veyrina's spine. Elyndra stiffened beside her, her eyes narrowing as she scanned the surrounding landscape.

"What was that?" Veyrina asked, her voice tight with tension.

"I don't know," Elyndra replied, her tone cautious. "But I don't like it."

Before Veyrina could respond, a figure emerged from the mist that had been swirling around them. At first, it was just a silhouette, a dark shape moving through the fog, but as it drew closer, the figure became clearer—a woman, tall and regal, her movements graceful but purposeful. She wore a long, flowing robe of dark green, embroidered with symbols Veyrina didn't recognize. Her hair was silver, shining like moonlight, and her eyes were a deep, piercing blue that seemed to see straight through them.

Elyndra's breath hitched when she saw the woman, her face paling as she took a step back. "No… it can't be."

The woman's lips curved into a knowing smile as she approached them. "It can, Elyndra," she said, her voice soft but commanding. "It's time."

Veyrina's eyes flicked between Elyndra and the stranger, confusion clouding her thoughts. "Who is she?" she asked, her voice shaky.

The woman's gaze shifted to Veyrina, her eyes locking onto hers with an intensity that sent a chill down her spine. "I am the one who has watched over you both," she said, her voice heavy with unspoken weight. "I am Veyrina's mother."

Veyrina's breath caught in her throat. Her mind spun in disbelief. "My… mother?"

Elyndra's expression faltered for a moment, her face a mixture of shock and something else—something dark and painful. She stepped closer to Veyrina, her hand brushing against hers in a fleeting moment of comfort.

The woman—Veyrina's mother—nodded solemnly. "Yes, child. You've been searching for answers, and I've been waiting for you. But the time for explanations is short."

Veyrina's heart raced, her thoughts a chaotic whirlwind. "What are you talking about?" she asked, her voice thick with emotion. "Why are you here? Why didn't you tell me before?"

Her mother's gaze softened, a deep sadness settling into the lines of her face. "I've been bound by the curse," she said, her voice tinged with regret. "The same curse that binds you both. You were never meant to remember. Not until now."

Elyndra stepped forward, her voice trembling with urgency. "What curse? What are you talking about?"

Veyrina's mother met her gaze, her eyes darkening. "The curse of forbidden love. A bond that was never meant to be. It was woven into your souls long ago, and now, it has begun to unravel."

Veyrina's breath caught in her throat. Her mind reeled with the implications of what her mother was saying. "Forbidden love? What do you mean?"

Her mother looked to the sky, her expression haunted. "The realm tests you. It tests your desires, your choices. The bond between you both is stronger than you realize. But it was never meant to be."

The words hung in the air, heavy with meaning. Veyrina's heart raced as she tried to make sense of the puzzle that was slowly coming together. Her mother's presence only deepened the mystery—she had been a part of this, and yet, she had remained silent for so long.

"You must choose," her mother continued, her voice dropping to a whisper. "The love that binds you is both a blessing and a curse. You can either embrace it, knowing that it will change everything, or walk away from each other, breaking the bond forever."

Veyrina's pulse quickened as the weight of the decision pressed down on her. The air seemed to hum with tension, the very fabric of the realm shifting in response to the choices before them. Her eyes flicked to Elyndra, who was standing beside her, her face a mixture of fear and determination.

"Which will you choose?" Veyrina's mother asked, her voice echoing with a finality that sent a chill through Veyrina's very soul.

The silence between them was suffocating, and Veyrina could feel the weight of her mother's words pressing down on her chest, making it hard to breathe. The choice that had been laid before them—embrace the love that had once bound them, or sever it forever—was one she wasn't ready to make. She had spent so long lost in the echoes of the past, struggling to understand who she was, where she came from. Now, the very essence of her being was at stake.

She turned to Elyndra, her heart pounding in her chest. The longing that had built between them over the past days was undeniable, yet the fear was equally potent. How could she trust this feeling? How could she trust herself?

Elyndra's gaze locked onto hers, and in that moment, it felt as though they were the only two beings left in the universe. The bond between them—the echo that had led them here, to this precipice—was undeniable. And yet, doubt lingered like a shadow, darkening the edges of the connection that had begun to bloom between them.

"Veyrina…" Elyndra whispered, her voice laced with uncertainty. "Do you believe her? Do you believe that we were meant to be?"

Veyrina swallowed hard, trying to find the right words. "I don't know. I don't know what's real anymore." Her voice trembled as she spoke, the weight of the unknown settling heavily on her shoulders. "But I know I can't walk away from you."

Elyndra's eyes softened, but the flicker of doubt remained. "But if we embrace this—if we give in to what's between us— what will happen to us? What will happen to this realm? To everything we've fought for?"

Veyrina reached out, her hand brushing against Elyndra's, feeling the warmth of her skin. "We don't have all the answers, but we can't keep running from it. We can't keep hiding from what's inside of us."

The sorceress—Veyrina's mother—watched them in silence, her expression unreadable. Finally, she spoke, her voice low and filled with quiet sorrow. "I've watched you both struggle, and I know the path ahead is fraught with danger. But you must understand something crucial."

Both women turned to face her, their attention riveted on the ancient sorceress.

"The realm you find yourselves in is not a place of simple choices," her mother continued. "It is a mirror of your hearts. The shadows and light you see around you—the temptation, the desire, the fear—are not just reflections of this world, but of what is within you. The bond between you two is more than just a connection forged in time—it is the very essence of this realm."

Veyrina felt a shiver run down her spine. "What do you mean?"

Her mother's eyes darkened, a deep sadness filling them. "This realm has a will of its own. It tests those who are connected by its power. If you are to truly embrace what lies between you, you will be forced to confront the deepest parts of yourselves—parts that even you do not fully understand."

Elyndra stepped forward, her eyes narrowing. "And what happens if we fail?"

Veyrina's mother's gaze hardened. "Then you will destroy each other. The bond between you will collapse, and this realm will collapse with it."

The words hung in the air like a curse, heavy and foreboding.

Veyrina felt her stomach twist in a knot. What choice did they really have? How could they know what was truly at stake?

"But we're not the only ones affected," Veyrina said, her voice breaking through the tense silence. "What about the people in this realm? What about everything we've seen?"

Her mother's lips tightened into a thin line, her expression softening for a moment as she looked at Veyrina. "The realm is a reflection of the balance between light and shadow, love and loss. Your connection, as dangerous as it may be, is the key to that balance. If you embrace it fully, you can restore what has been broken. If not…"

She didn't finish the sentence, but the implication was clear.

Veyrina turned her gaze to Elyndra, her heart hammering in her chest. She could feel the desire, the pull between them, so strong now it was almost unbearable. The emotions she had kept buried for so long were bubbling to the surface, demanding release. But she knew—deep down—that giving in to this desire was not a simple thing. It would change everything.

"I don't want to hurt anyone," Veyrina said quietly, her voice barely audible. "I don't want to destroy this place, or us."

Elyndra reached out, her fingers brushing against Veyrina's again, and this time, the touch lingered. "We don't have to do this alone," she said softly. "We're in this together. Whatever happens, we face it as one."

A surge of warmth flooded Veyrina's chest at her words. They had been through so much together already, and the thought of losing Elyndra—of not being able to face the challenges ahead by her side—was unbearable.

Her mother stepped back, her eyes closing as she seemed to sense the gravity of their decision. "You will find the answers you seek. But remember this: the choices you make will shape not only your fate but the fate of this realm as well. Choose wisely."

With those final words, she disappeared into the mist, leaving Veyrina and Elyndra alone, standing on the edge of an abyss they could not yet see. The tension between them was palpable, a thread of emotion pulling them together while fear and uncertainty threatened to tear them apart.

Elyndra turned to face Veyrina fully now, her expression softening. She reached out, her hands trembling slightly, and cupped Veyrina's face in her palms. "I don't know what will happen next. But I know I don't want to lose you. Not again."

Veyrina closed her eyes, leaning into Elyndra's touch, feeling the heat of her skin, the warmth that radiated from her like a beacon in the darkness. "I don't want to lose you either."

The space between them seemed to collapse in on itself, and before Veyrina could fully comprehend what was happening, Elyndra leaned in, her lips brushing gently against hers. The kiss was soft at first, tentative, as though neither of them were sure what to expect. But as the seconds stretched into eternity, the kiss deepened, a surge of desire and longing flooding their senses. It was as though the entire realm had fallen away, leaving only the two of them in this moment of fragile connection.

When they finally pulled away, breathless and shaken, Veyrina's mind raced. She had given in to the pull, the desire that had been simmering beneath the surface, but now she was more uncertain than ever. What did this mean? What would happen next?

But there was no time to dwell on those questions now. The echoes had grown louder once again, calling them forward.

The realm was shifting, changing, and there was no going back.

"We have to keep moving," Veyrina said, her voice thick with emotion.

Elyndra nodded, her eyes dark with the same uncertainty, but there was a new fire in her gaze—one that matched Veyrina's own.

Together, they turned toward the horizon, the echoes of their past—and their future—guiding them forward into the unknown.

Six

The Betrayal Within

The path ahead seemed to stretch endlessly before them. The echo of their past still reverberated through the air, but now, it was tinged with uncertainty. Veyrina could feel it—the change in the air, the subtle shift in Elyndra's demeanor, the way the silence between them had grown heavier since they kissed. Her heart, once sure in its resolve, now trembled with the weight of unspoken words, of things that lay buried in the shadows of their shared history.

They walked side by side, the sound of their footsteps muffled on the soft earth beneath them. The mist had thickened, curling around their ankles like tendrils, as if the realm itself was alive, watching, waiting.

Elyndra had been distant lately. The pull of their bond—the shared connection that had once been so powerful—now seemed frayed at the edges. Veyrina couldn't understand it. Elyndra's touch had been soft, reassuring, but something in her eyes held back, as if she were guarding a secret that was slipping further away with every passing moment.

And then, just as Veyrina thought she might speak her mind, they reached a clearing.

At the heart of the clearing stood an imposing figure, a silhouette etched in the mist. Tall, broad-shouldered, a dark cloak that billowed like smoke. His face was obscured by the shadows, but the unmistakable feeling of recognition gnawed at Veyrina's gut. She stepped forward, her pulse quickening, but Elyndra's hand shot out, gripping her wrist firmly.

"Stay back," Elyndra said, her voice tight with warning.

The figure stepped forward into the mist's clearing, and Veyrina felt the ground beneath her feet shudder. The stranger's eyes gleamed through the veil of his hood, a sharp, calculating glint that froze her where she stood. The man—no, *the ghost*—was not unfamiliar. It was Zevianne Althros. Elyndra's past.

The name echoed in Veyrina's mind, a whisper of a past life, of pain and love lost. She tried to suppress the surge of jealousy that clawed at her chest, but it was impossible. She didn't want to feel it—didn't want to let it control her—but the tension in the air made her heart race.

Zevianne spoke, his voice smooth as silk, carrying a dark, dangerous undertone. "Elyndra," he said, his gaze flicking toward her. "It's been a long time. I see you've moved on." He turned his attention to Veyrina, the intensity of his gaze almost unbearable. "Or perhaps, you've been *moved on*."

The words struck like a blow, and Veyrina felt herself stagger, but Elyndra was already stepping in front of her, as though she could shield her from the weight of his words. "Zevianne, this is not the time—"

"Oh, but it *is* the time, Elyndra." Zevianne's voice was low, and Veyrina could see the flicker of something bitter in his eyes. "For her to understand what she's really gotten herself into."

Veyrina's pulse quickened as she took a step back, but Elyndra held her ground, her jaw clenched, her fists curled at her sides. "What are you doing here, Zevianne?"

"I've come to make sure she understands." He paused, the cruel smile on his lips tightening. "I'm afraid the truth isn't as simple as she believes."

Veyrina's mind raced. She glanced between the two, sensing the shift in the air. The echoes seemed to grow louder, swirling around them like a storm. But the words Zevianne spoke were even louder still, shaking the ground beneath her feet.

"You think this is love?" he asked, his eyes cutting through Elyndra's defenses, turning them into a distant memory. "What you feel for her, it's nothing more than a curse, Elyndra. A curse that was *never meant to be broken*. This... this bond you share? It was created to keep you apart."

Veyrina's breath hitched. The words didn't make sense—*a curse*—but the way Zevianne said them, the certainty in his voice, made her doubt everything. She turned to Elyndra, who stood frozen, her eyes wide, her face pale. "Is that true?" she whispered, her voice trembling.

Elyndra shook her head, the tension in her shoulders tight. "Veyrina, no, it's—"

But Zevianne cut her off with a sharp laugh. "You've forgotten so much, haven't you? The truth lies in the shadows of the past, waiting to be uncovered. Don't you remember? Don't you remember why we were separated? *Why you were cursed?*" He stepped closer, his gaze fixed on Veyrina. "This love between you two? It was never meant to flourish. It was meant to *tear you apart.*"

Veyrina's stomach twisted with a mixture of fear and disbelief. "No," she whispered, stepping back. "That's not true. It can't be."

But the doubt gnawed at her heart, and she couldn't stop herself from looking at Elyndra, as though seeking the answers in her eyes. Elyndra's eyes flickered, but her lips remained pressed together in silence. The weight of Zevianne's words lingered in the space between them, thickening the air.

Zevianne took a step toward Veyrina, his presence looming, his dark energy pressing down on her like a weight. "You don't understand. *You never will.* Elyndra and I—" He hesitated, as though savoring the moment, before he finally spoke again, his voice cold. "We were once bound together by something much greater than love. A power so ancient, so primal, that even the realm trembled before it."

Veyrina shook her head, feeling the anger surge inside of her. "You're lying."

"No," Elyndra said softly, stepping forward, her voice shaking. "He's not. It's true. The curse… it was meant to break us apart, to make sure we never stood together again. But I never wanted it. I never wanted to lose you, Veyrina."

The words broke something inside of Veyrina. She felt as if the ground had opened beneath her feet, swallowing everything she thought she knew. "Then why didn't you tell me? Why didn't you—" She cut herself off, not wanting to accuse her, not wanting to push her further into the shadows of the past.

Elyndra's eyes softened with guilt. "I didn't remember… until now. Until it all came rushing back."

Zevianne laughed again, a cold, mocking sound that sent shivers down Veyrina's spine. "How convenient," he said. "Elyndra always was a master at hiding the truth, burying it deep so that it would never come to the surface."

Veyrina looked at Elyndra, searching her face for the woman she had fallen in love with, the woman who had stood beside her through every trial. The woman who was supposed to be her partner, her equal. "Why didn't you tell me the truth?"

"I didn't remember!" Elyndra cried, her voice desperate. "I swear, Veyrina, I didn't remember until now. The curse made sure of it. It twisted everything inside me, keeping the truth locked away."

Veyrina's heart wrenched at the anguish in Elyndra's voice, but the doubt—the seed of suspicion that Zevianne had planted—continued to fester inside her. "And you expect me to just *believe* you? After everything?"

Elyndra took a step forward, her voice barely a whisper. "I'm asking you to trust me. Please."

But the crack in their bond—the rupture caused by the lies, the half-truths—was wide and growing. And no matter how much Veyrina wanted to trust Elyndra, the shadows of the past lingered too close, too powerful, to ignore.

Zevianne stepped back, his smirk spreading wider. "You'll see, Veyrina. You'll see soon enough."

And with that, the figure melted back into the mist, leaving Veyrina and Elyndra standing together, but miles apart, their hearts pulled in two different directions.

Veyrina stood in the clearing, her breath shallow, her chest tight. Zevianne had vanished into the mist, but his words clung to her like a curse of their own. A curse designed to tear them apart. The thought alone sent a tremor through her body.

She turned to Elyndra, who was standing a few paces away, her face drained of color. Elyndra's usually steadfast demeanor had cracked, and in her eyes—those familiar eyes—Veyrina saw the storm. The internal battle of someone caught between past and present, between the truth they desperately wanted to keep buried and the future they longed to embrace.

Elyndra spoke first, her voice hoarse. "I never wanted this. I never wanted him to come back."

Veyrina's heart skipped a beat. "But you know him. You knew him—what *he* just said. It's all true, isn't it?"

Elyndra flinched as if struck, then took a slow step toward her. "Veyrina, please, I—"

But Veyrina stepped back, shaking her head. "You've been keeping so much from me. You say you didn't remember, but how can I believe you now?"

Elyndra's eyes flashed with pain, and for a brief moment, Veyrina saw the rawness of her emotions—the guilt, the fear. It was almost too much to bear.

"I didn't remember. Not until recently. Not until all of this—" Elyndra gestured toward the endless mist, the shadowy landscape around them, "came rushing back. The memories... the curse—it's like a fog that clouds everything. Zevianne and I—we were bound together long before I met you. It wasn't just love, Veyrina. It was... *destiny*. But it was never meant to last. The curse was placed on us long ago, designed to make sure our hearts were torn apart. I never wanted to hurt you."

Veyrina could hear the desperation in Elyndra's voice, but it only made the anger burn hotter. "Why didn't you tell me sooner?" Her words came out in a harsh whisper, a challenge. "Why let it go on like this, all the while hiding the truth from me?"

Elyndra took another step forward, her eyes pleading. "I wanted to protect you from it. I never wanted you to suffer because of this curse. I thought if we were strong enough, we could break it, that we could create a future without the shadow of the past haunting us."

"But Zevianne—" Veyrina's voice cracked as the fury rose, "he's been playing us. Manipulating everything."

"I know," Elyndra whispered, her gaze dropping. "He's always had a way of twisting the truth, of manipulating the feelings of those around him. But that doesn't change the fact that the curse is real."

Veyrina's mind spun. The memories, the feelings—the ones that had been so simple and pure before Zevianne's intrusion—were now clouded by doubt. The echoes that connected her to Elyndra were still there, but the shadows that lingered in the corners of her heart grew deeper. She didn't know if she could trust the woman in front of her. Could she trust her own heart?

The silence stretched between them, an impenetrable wall. Veyrina could feel the weight of the decision pressing down on her. Should she believe Elyndra, or was she just another pawn in a cruel game devised by fate, by Zevianne's machinations?

"I don't know what to believe anymore," Veyrina said, her voice trembling. "I want to trust you, Elyndra, but I don't know how."

Elyndra reached for her, but Veyrina stepped back, the distance between them suddenly feeling like miles. She felt raw, exposed. "I don't want to be a part of some cursed destiny. I *chose* to be with you, Elyndra. I chose to trust you."

"I never asked you to choose," Elyndra said quietly, her own pain evident. "I never wanted you to be dragged into this. But now… now that you know the truth, you have to make a choice. We can either fight it, or we can let the curse take us."

The gravity of her words hung in the air like an oppressive weight. Fight the curse or succumb to it. The path before Veyrina seemed narrow, with no easy way forward.

A voice echoed through her mind—Zevianna's words, like a poison leaking into her thoughts: *This love was never meant to last.*

Could they really fight it? Or was it inevitable, like the tides pulling them apart no matter how hard they tried to stay afloat?

Veyrina's head ached. She closed her eyes, trying to steady herself. She reached into her chest, seeking the strength, the certainty that had once been there. When her eyes opened, the mist around them seemed to blur, swirling with her thoughts, turning everything into a haze.

"I don't know if I can fight this anymore, Elyndra." The words were barely a whisper, but the weight of them felt suffocating. "I thought I understood this bond, but now… now I don't know what's real."

"Please don't say that." Elyndra's voice was soft, her eyes pleading. "I swear to you, I'm not lying to you. Everything we've shared, everything we've felt—it's real. The curse may be ancient, but it's not stronger than us. We can overcome it, if we stand together."

Veyrina shook her head slowly, still not looking at Elyndra.

"I don't know if I can trust you anymore. I don't know if I can trust *myself.*"

Elyndra's breath caught, and for a moment, she looked as though the world had collapsed around her. She stepped back, her face hardening into something unreadable. "So this is it then. This is how it ends?"

Veyrina closed her eyes, swallowing against the sudden surge of tears. She didn't know. She didn't have the answers, and the silence between them felt like a chasm that could never be crossed.

The wind picked up, rustling the mist, carrying with it the faintest trace of something far darker. A foreboding sense of inevitability seemed to pulse through the air. It was as though the realm itself was watching, waiting for them to choose.

Finally, Elyndra turned and began to walk away. "I won't force you to decide now. But know this—no matter what happens, no matter where the echoes take us, I will always love you."

Veyrina watched her retreat, the words she longed to say caught in her throat. She felt the world shifting around her, the weight of a thousand emotions pressing against her chest, suffocating her. She didn't know what to believe anymore.

The moment stretched, a fragile thread between them.

And then, with a final glance over her shoulder, Elyndra disappeared into the mist, leaving Veyrina alone, with nothing but the whispers of the past to guide her forward.

Veyrina stood there, breathless, the weight of the decision pressing on her heart. The echoes were louder now, swirling with both doubt and longing. A sharp pain coursed through her chest, and for a moment, she wondered if it was the curse tightening its grip, or if it was something else—something deeper, something even more dangerous.

The fog seemed to deepen around her as the sun began to dip below the horizon. And with it, the world fell into shadow, leaving her to face the impossible choice that lay ahead.

Would she fight for love?

Or would the past—its curse—consume them both?

Seven

A Time Without End

The air inside the hidden archive felt ancient—thick with dust and time. The walls of the chamber rose high around them, lined with shelves that stretched beyond sight, filled with scrolls, tomes, and artifacts that hadn't seen the light of day in centuries. It was a place untouched by the world outside, a place where the echoes of the past whispered in every crevice, in every corner.

Veyrina and Elyndra stood in the center of it, the weight of their discovery pressing down on them like a heavy fog. The map they had followed, the path that had brought them here, now seemed like a dream. Nothing had prepared them for this.

"Do you think this is it?" Veyrina asked, her voice soft but filled with the sharp edge of tension. "The answers we've been searching for?"

Elyndra didn't answer immediately. She stood frozen, her gaze scanning the vastness of the archive, taking in the staggering array of knowledge hidden within the walls. Every inch of the room felt alive with the stories of their past. Of their countless lives. Of the cycle they could never escape.

"I don't know," Elyndra finally said, her voice hollow. "But it's the only lead we have left."

They moved deeper into the archive, the floor creaking beneath their steps, the air heavy with the scent of old paper and wood. The silence was oppressive, suffocating even. It was as if the very air around them held its breath, waiting for them to uncover what lay hidden in the darkness.

At the far end of the room, a large stone pedestal stood, and atop it rested a single, weathered tome. The cover was dark, nearly black, with symbols etched into its surface—symbols that seemed to pulse with a faint light, as if they were alive.

Veyrina reached for it, her fingers brushing against the cool stone. Her pulse quickened, a strange energy thrumming through her veins, making the hairs on the back of her neck stand on end. This was it—the final piece of the puzzle. The answers they had been desperately searching for.

But as her hand made contact with the book, a cold shiver ran down her spine. The air seemed to grow thicker, the very atmosphere pressing in on them. A distant, echoing sound filled the room—a low, mournful hum, like the wail of a forgotten memory. It was the sound of time, a sound that twisted and turned, bending the fabric of reality itself.

The book trembled under her touch, and with a sharp gasp, Veyrina pulled her hand back. Her eyes met Elyndra's, wide with the same fear and awe.

"This is it," Elyndra whispered, her voice barely audible.

Together, they moved closer, their steps careful, almost reverent. Veyrina hesitated for only a moment before opening the tome. The pages inside were ancient, brittle to the touch, and the words seemed to shimmer as if alive, flickering between languages and symbols, a testament to the forgotten knowledge within.

Veyrina's breath caught as her eyes skimmed the text. Words danced before her, impossibly old, yet undeniably familiar. *The cycle of love... the curse of time...*

"This can't be real," Veyrina murmured, her voice trembling. "Is this… our story?"

Elyndra stepped closer, her face pale as she leaned over to read the words alongside Veyrina. As they both read, the ancient tale of their love unfolded before them—words of a bond so deep that it transcended time itself, echoing through countless lives and worlds.

"Two souls, bound by fate, condemned to relive their love with every passing age, each time a new beginning, each time a painful end. Their love, eternal as it was, would never be free. The realm that trapped them, a force beyond comprehension, would erase their memories with each cycle, keeping them bound in an endless loop. The curse could only be broken through sacrifice, a choice neither was ever willing to make..."

Veyrina stopped reading, her throat tight. The weight of the words hung in the air, suffocating her. Their love. Their bond. It was not new. It had never been new. It had been *repeating*. Over and over. Each time, they were brought together, only to lose each other again, with the price always the same—*their memories*.

"I don't… I don't understand," Elyndra said, her voice strangled with disbelief. "How is this possible?"

Veyrina closed the book with a forceful snap, her hands shaking as she placed it back on the pedestal. The echoes of the past pulsed in the air around them, the weight of history pressing in on them. Their love had never been a gift—it had been a curse, a cycle they were trapped in. Every time they had found each other, they had lost the very essence of what made them who they were. And this time… this time was no different.

"The realm," Elyndra whispered, her voice breaking. "It's the one controlling us. It's keeping us from breaking free."

Veyrina stepped back, her eyes wide with horror. "It's not just the curse, is it? It's the realm itself. It's been orchestrating all of this—our love, our separation. Every time, it erases everything. Everything we've ever felt, everything we've built together."

"But why?" Elyndra asked, her voice raw. "Why would it do that? Why would it take away what's real?"

Veyrina shook her head, feeling the weight of her thoughts like a crushing tide. "I don't know. But if we're trapped in this… if we're meant to be cursed forever, then what chance do we have? What choice is left for us?"

A heavy silence filled the air as the weight of their predicament sank in. The echoes—their bond—were undeniable, but they were also the very thing keeping them bound to this twisted cycle. Each time they had loved, each time they had fought to stay together, it had always ended in heartbreak. In loss. And the memories, the moments they had shared, would always be erased.

"We can't keep doing this," Veyrina said, her voice barely above a whisper. "We can't keep fighting a cycle that was never meant to be broken."

Elyndra looked up at her, her eyes filled with something like sorrow. "I know. But it's not just the love that's keeping us here. It's the *realm* itself. And if we break the cycle, if we break the curse… we lose everything."

The room seemed to pulse with an energy that Veyrina could almost taste. The weight of the decision before them was unbearable. The love they had shared—it was everything. And yet, the cost of that love was also everything.

"The only way out…" Elyndra began, her voice faltering. "Is to sacrifice the love we have. To let it go. To choose to end it, forever."

The words hung in the air like a death sentence, the finality of it hitting Veyrina with a force she hadn't been prepared for. She took a step back, the air in the room growing thick and heavy.

Sacrifice. To break the cycle, they would have to choose to sever the very thing that had bound them together for so long. The thought of it made her chest ache, her heart thrumming with a pain that was almost unbearable. To lose Elyndra, to lose this—this love—was something she couldn't fathom. Yet, the more she thought about it, the clearer it became.

Their love could not be the one thing that brought them both to ruin.

But could she let go?

Could Elyndra?

The echoes of the past seemed to echo louder now, the past, present, and future tangled in a tangle of light and shadow. And in the heart of the archive, with the truth laid bare before them, Veyrina and Elyndra were left to face the impossible choice.

Would they break the cycle?

Or would they surrender to the love that had always torn them apart?

The silence between them stretched on, thick and suffocating, as Veyrina and Elyndra stood in the heart of the hidden archive. The weight of the decision they faced hung heavy in the air, a storm of emotions brewing on the cusp of their understanding. The ancient book lay open before them, its pages whispering secrets they had never been prepared to hear.

"How did we end up here?" Elyndra's voice was hoarse, the words laced with a desperation that tugged at Veyrina's heart. "How did we become trapped in this endless cycle? Why couldn't we have just… *chosen* differently?"

Veyrina's eyes searched Elyndra's face, a mixture of grief and confusion welling up inside her. The same questions had echoed in her mind since their first encounter, since the very moment they had realized their love had somehow transcended time, only to be lost over and over again. But now, standing on the precipice of a choice that could either release them or doom them forever, Veyrina was paralyzed by the enormity of it all.

"I don't know," she admitted softly. "But I can't keep living with the memory of a love that's always slipping away from me."

Her fingers trembled as she ran them over the edges of the tome. It was a cruel irony that the very thing that had held the key to their endless suffering was the same thing that could set them free. The choice, though clear, felt impossible.

Elyndra stepped forward, her presence a beacon of warmth in the chilling atmosphere. Her eyes were raw, filled with anguish. "Veyrina… do you think *I* haven't wanted to break free from this? To forget the pain, to forget the loss we keep reliving?"

Veyrina turned toward her, their gazes locking. There was

something in Elyndra's eyes that caught her breath, something that spoke of deep regret and untold sorrow. It was a look she had seen before, in countless lifetimes, but it was now that it seemed to hold the weight of a thousand years.

"You don't have to carry this alone," Elyndra whispered, her voice breaking through Veyrina's turbulent thoughts. "I've always carried it with you, and I will continue to do so. But this… This is beyond both of us."

The words struck like a physical blow. Veyrina felt a pang in her chest, as though her heart was being torn in two. The bond between them was undeniable—stronger than any force, any curse. But the realization of its true cost, the understanding that their love had always been a paradox, a beautiful tragedy, was suffocating.

"I don't want to lose you again, Elyndra," Veyrina confessed, her voice a whisper, filled with pain. "I can't."

Elyndra's lips quivered, a shadow of a smile flickering across her face before it vanished, leaving behind only the sorrow of centuries. "Then let me make this choice for both of us."

The words were like a soft caress, yet they felt like the sharpest blade. Veyrina didn't know what to say. Her throat tightened, but there was no air left to breathe.

"I can't let you do that," Veyrina replied, her voice barely audible. "If we're to end this cycle, we end it together. But it must be our choice—*both* of us. Not just yours."

Elyndra stepped back, her face etched with sadness. "But you're right. If we break the cycle, we lose everything—the love, the memories, all the moments that make us who we are. Do you really want to give all that up?"

The question echoed in Veyrina's mind like the toll of a bell, resounding through her chest with an unbearable weight. *Do*

I?

Her gaze flickered back to the tome, the words dancing before her eyes, a reminder of the curse they were bound to. Could she truly sacrifice everything—every moment of passion, every soft touch, every shared laugh—to escape the endless pain of their repeated separation?

The realm that had entrapped them was powerful, and its hold on them was unrelenting. But was it enough to destroy everything they had? Their love was a gift and a curse, but was it worth saving, even if it meant losing everything else?

Elyndra reached out, her hand trembling as it brushed against Veyrina's. The touch was gentle but urgent, as if the very act of touching was a lifeline in the sea of uncertainty between them.

"Veyrina, whatever choice we make, it's ours to bear. But it has to be made now."

Veyrina nodded, her pulse quickening. The air was charged with an energy she could almost taste, and her heart beat faster, louder, as if it knew the choice was inevitable. The time to decide had come. She could feel it—the weight of the past, the present, and the future pressing down on them both.

"I don't know if I'm strong enough to let go," Veyrina confessed, her voice trembling. "But I *do* know that I can't keep living in this endless cycle. I can't keep losing you. If it means losing everything—then maybe that's what we have to do."

The words were painful to speak, as though tearing something from her soul. Yet, beneath the pain, there was a spark of clarity. The love they had shared—endless, passionate, and fraught with pain—was not meant to be this way. They were not meant to suffer forever, to be trapped in this eternal loop of love and loss.

Elyndra squeezed her hand tighter, her own face pale but determined. "Then we fight. We fight the curse. Together."

And with those words, the final decision was made.

Veyrina could feel the very fabric of reality around them tremble as the air grew thick with magic, with the raw power of their choices, both the love they held and the sacrifice they were about to make. The echoes that had tied them together for so long—those soft, haunting voices from the past—began to wail in unison, louder and more insistent than ever before.

But this time, Veyrina didn't look away. This time, she faced the echoes head-on, and with Elyndra beside her, she knew they could finally break free.

She took a deep breath, steadying herself, and turned back to the tome. The answer was within the pages—hidden, but waiting for them to find it. The truth behind the curse, the final piece of the puzzle.

They weren't done yet. They still had a choice to make. And they would make it together, no matter the cost.

"I won't forget you, Elyndra," Veyrina whispered, the words holding more weight than any spell could.

Elyndra nodded, her hand tightening around hers. "And I will never forget you, no matter what happens."

As they prepared to face the final test, the magic in the air hummed louder, the realm itself seeming to tremble beneath them. And in that moment, Veyrina realized that their love, for all its pain, for all its losses, was the one thing that had kept them alive through every cycle. But now, it was time for the final choice to be made.

Would they give in to the curse, or would they finally break free?

Eight

The Keeper of Echoes

The air in the echo realm was thick with a haunting stillness, pressing in on Veyrina and Elyndra as they stood at the edge of the shimmering abyss. The echoes that had once called to them seemed now to reverberate from every corner of the ancient world. The pulsing vibrations of the realm twisted around them like a living, breathing entity, a constant reminder of the unrelenting cycle they were trapped in.

As they moved deeper into the heart of this place, the ground beneath their feet seemed to hum with each step they took. Veyrina's heart pounded in her chest, the pressure of their situation building with every moment. It felt as though something unseen watched them—something ancient and vast, pulling at the very fabric of their existence. The air was thick with magic, and as Veyrina's breath quickened, she could feel the walls of the echo realm pressing closer, suffocating them in its enigmatic embrace.

Then, as if conjured by the very force of their shared turmoil, a figure appeared before them. At first, it was only a whisper of shadow, a distortion in the air, but slowly, it solidified into a presence—a figure draped in an ethereal cloak woven from the very fabric of time. The Keeper of Echoes.

The figure stood tall, their face hidden beneath a hood that cast a veil of darkness. But there was no mistaking the presence of the being, ancient beyond measure, as old as the echo realm itself. Their voice, when it finally came, resonated like a thousand voices speaking in unison.

"You have come," the Keeper intoned, their words vibrating through the air like a soundwave that seemed to settle in the marrow of their bones. "The echo is relentless, and yet you seek to break its hold. But be warned, for the price of freedom is high."

Veyrina's gaze flickered to Elyndra, her heart heavy with the weight of their journey thus far. The truth about their connection, their love, their curse—it was all so overwhelming. How many times had they been here before? How many times had the echo called them to this very place, only for them to lose each other in the end?

"What price?" Veyrina asked, her voice barely above a whisper. Her hand reached instinctively for Elyndra's, seeking some comfort, some reminder that they were in this together, no matter what the Keeper offered.

The Keeper's eyes glowed faintly beneath the hood, two pinpricks of light in the suffocating darkness. "There is always a price," the Keeper replied, stepping forward, their form now tangible in the air between them. The ground beneath their feet began to pulse, as though alive with the weight of the decision ahead.

"The price of your freedom is forgetting," the Keeper continued, their tone shifting, as though they were revealing a long-guarded secret. "You may live in eternal bliss, free from the echoes of the past. But in doing so, you will forget the love that binds you. The very memories of each other, the pain of loss and the joy of reunion—it will all vanish, like a fleeting dream, leaving only an empty existence."

Veyrina felt her breath catch in her throat. The thought of erasing the love she shared with Elyndra—the deep, abiding connection that had been her anchor in the storm—was unfathomable. But the Keeper's words held an undeniable pull, a quiet temptation she couldn't ignore. To live without the curse, without the weight of their fractured memories—it was a life that called to her, promising peace and solace.

Elyndra, too, seemed caught in the web of the Keeper's words. Her brow furrowed in thought, her eyes searching Veyrina's face for any sign of what she should do. The tension between them was palpable, each woman wrestling with the same question, the same fear: could they really forget everything, even the love that had bound them?

Veyrina's grip on Elyndra's hand tightened, a silent plea for them to hold on to what they had. The truth of their bond, the depth of their love—it was real, it was theirs. Could they truly erase it? Could they truly allow themselves to live without it?

"And what of the other option?" Elyndra spoke, her voice low and hesitant. "What happens if we don't choose your offer?"

The Keeper's cloak shimmered, and they took a step closer, their presence overwhelming, as though the very air around them was charged with power. "If you refuse the offer of bliss," the Keeper said, their voice now tinged with an edge of something darker, "you will face the full weight of your curse. The echoes will continue, and you will remain trapped in an endless cycle, unable to escape. Your love will be your prison, and each time you are torn apart, the wounds will grow deeper. You will be bound to this realm forever."

Veyrina's heart raced at the implications of the Keeper's words. The very thought of being trapped in an eternal cycle of pain, of losing Elyndra time and time again—her chest tightened at the prospect. And yet, the alternative was just as terrifying: living in a world without their love, without the memories of the bond that had once defined them.

"You ask us to choose between forgetting and suffering," Veyrina said, her voice steady despite the chaos swirling within her. "But what of the third option? Is there no way to escape the cycle without losing everything?"

The Keeper's eyes gleamed with an unsettling knowledge, as though they had been waiting for that very question. "There is a way," the Keeper replied, their voice dropping to a whisper. "But it comes at a cost far greater than anything you have yet imagined."

Veyrina felt the hairs on the back of her neck stand on end, a chill creeping down her spine. "What is it?" she demanded, unable to keep the desperation from her voice. "Tell us what we must do."

The Keeper's hand, long and bony, reached out to touch the air before them, as though drawing an invisible line in the ether. "To truly break the cycle, you must sever the very essence of your bond. The love that ties you together must be destroyed—obliterated, so that it can never return. Only then will the echoes cease, and the realm will release you. You will be free."

The words hung in the air like a death sentence, and for a moment, neither Veyrina nor Elyndra could speak. The thought of destroying their love, of willingly letting go of the bond that had brought them together—it was a horrific thought, an impossible one. How could they do such a thing? How could they live without each other?

The Keeper's gaze held them both, unblinking, as though waiting for their response. The silence stretched between them, thick with the weight of the decision that lay ahead.

Veyrina's mind whirled, her heart aching with the very thought of what the Keeper was asking. She couldn't—no, she wouldn't—give up on them. She couldn't allow their love to be destroyed, not when it had been the only thing that had ever felt truly real in this fractured existence.

But Elyndra's expression had shifted, her brow furrowed as she stepped closer to Veyrina. "Is there no other way?" Elyndra's voice trembled, her fingers brushing lightly against Veyrina's. "I can't lose you again, Veyrina. I won't."

The words struck a chord deep within Veyrina, the truth of Elyndra's feelings mirroring her own. They had come this far together—how could they walk away now?

The Keeper remained silent, watching them with an unreadable expression. The weight of the decision hung heavy in the air, pressing down on them both.

Finally, Veyrina spoke, her voice firm but filled with a quiet resolve. "We will find another way. We will break the cycle, but not at the cost of our love. There has to be another path."

Elyndra's eyes met hers, a glimmer of hope flickering there. She nodded slowly, her voice barely a whisper. "Together."

The Keeper's gaze flickered with a faint, almost imperceptible sigh, as though they had expected this response. "Very well," they said, their voice echoing ominously. "But remember—should you fail, the consequences will be dire. You will be trapped forever in the echoes, lost to each other for eternity."

With those final words, the Keeper began to fade into the shadow, their form dissolving into the mist of the echo realm.

As the figure disappeared, the silence returned, leaving Veyrina and Elyndra alone once more. The weight of the decision they had just made settled over them, but beneath the tension, a spark of hope flickered between them, the first light in what had been an endless night. Together, they would find a way to break the cycle.

But in the distance, the echo of their love pulsed louder, a warning that their journey was far from over.

The moment the Keeper's presence dissolved into the swirling shadows of the realm, an eerie stillness enveloped Veyrina and Elyndra. The air, once thick with the weight of their encounter, now felt impossibly quiet, as if the very essence of the echo realm held its breath. Neither spoke immediately, their minds reeling from the gravity of the decision they had just made.

Elyndra took a slow, deliberate step toward Veyrina, her hand reaching out to gently rest on her shoulder. It was a soft touch, but there was a weight to it—a weight of shared understanding, shared fear, and an unspoken promise. Together, they would face whatever lay ahead.

"I… I don't know what we're walking into, Veyrina," Elyndra whispered, her voice thick with emotion. "But I can't imagine a life without you. Not even in a world without the echoes. It's not worth it."

Veyrina felt her heart break at the depth of Elyndra's words. She had known, in her core, that they would never choose the path of forgetting, that the love they shared was not something to be discarded. The mere thought of losing it was unthinkable. But Elyndra's words brought clarity, making the decision feel even more impossible. They were now on a path that would either lead to freedom or their destruction.

Veyrina turned to face Elyndra fully, her hand clasping the other woman's tightly. "We'll find a way to break the cycle. We have to. We've come too far, and we've fought too hard to lose each other now."

The resonance of her words reverberated in the air, filling the space between them with the certainty of a shared vow. Yet, beneath that certainty, a nagging doubt lingered. Would they truly succeed? Could they really break free from the echoes, from the cruel cycle that had bound them for centuries? Or were they simply setting themselves up for more pain, more loss?

A distant cry echoed through the realm, faint and haunting, as though mocking their resolve. It was the sound of the echoes, reminding them of their place in this world—reminding them that they had been trapped here before, and would be trapped again if they failed.

Without another word, they began to walk forward, the path ahead lit by the faint, flickering light of their bond, casting long shadows on the ground. Each step seemed to carry the weight of the past, the weight of every life they had shared and lost. Yet, there was a certain determination in their steps, a quiet force that pushed them forward. They had made their choice.

As they moved deeper into the realm, the air grew colder, and the landscape shifted subtly around them. What had once been a space of vast, ethereal beauty now seemed darker, more oppressive. The shimmering lights that had filled the air began to dim, and the very ground beneath their feet seemed to pulse with an ominous energy.

A low rumble echoed from ahead, and the ground trembled beneath them. It was as if the realm itself was responding to their defiance. The very walls seemed to close in, tightening around them, threatening to engulf them in the very same cycle they had sworn to break.

Then, a shape appeared in the distance—a figure, standing in the middle of the path, bathed in a pale light. It was tall and imposing, cloaked in shadows that seemed to shift and flicker like flame. For a moment, neither Veyrina nor Elyndra moved. They only stared, the tension between them mounting with every passing second.

"Another test?" Elyndra murmured, her voice filled with a mixture of dread and resolve.

Veyrina nodded. She didn't need to speak—she could feel it too. This was no coincidence. The realm was testing them again, forcing them to confront their resolve. And this figure, whatever it was, was the next trial they would face.

The figure moved, its form shifting with a fluidity that defied logic. It glided toward them, and Veyrina felt her pulse quicken. Her instincts screamed at her to be ready for anything, but she had no idea what to expect. The figure stopped just a few feet in front of them, its presence towering, and yet there was something strangely serene about it, as if it held the answers they sought.

"You have chosen to defy the realm," the figure's voice boomed, the sound vibrating through the ground and resonating deep within their chests. "You have chosen to risk everything, even your love. But do you understand the cost?"

Veyrina's heart sank. The question felt like a challenge, one designed to tear at their resolve. She looked to Elyndra, who met her gaze with a firm expression, one that reflected the same determination Veyrina felt deep in her soul.

"We understand," Veyrina replied, her voice unwavering. "We're willing to face whatever comes next. We've already lost so much—we won't lose each other again."

The figure seemed to pause, as if considering her words. The air around them thickened, and for a moment, Veyrina could almost feel the weight of time itself pressing in on them. The echoes, the realm, and the cycle—they were all interconnected, woven together by a force that was beyond their understanding. The figure's eyes glowed, burning with a knowing light that made her feel small, insignificant.

"Then you will face the trial," the figure said, its voice low and measured. "But be warned—the cost of breaking the cycle is greater than you realize. The very nature of your love is bound to this realm, and if you succeed, it will cease to exist as you know it. The echoes will be no more. But the love you seek to preserve will be sacrificed."

The words hung in the air, heavy with the weight of their implication. Veyrina's breath caught in her throat, and she felt her pulse race. Sacrificing their love? The very thing they had fought for, the very thing that had defined them for eternity?

"No," Elyndra whispered, shaking her head. "That's not possible. There has to be another way. We can't lose what we've built."

The figure remained unmoved, its gaze fixed upon them. "This is the price of freedom," it said, its voice now softer, but no less chilling. "Do you still wish to proceed?"

Veyrina's mind raced, her thoughts a chaotic whirlwind of fear and defiance. How could they face such a choice? The love they had shared across time—was it truly worth the cost of their very existence? Could they live without each other, even if it meant breaking free from the cycle that had bound them?

She looked to Elyndra again, searching her face for any sign of doubt, any sign that they should turn back. But all she saw in Elyndra's eyes was a reflection of her own fear and resolve. Together, they had made this decision. Together, they would face whatever came next.

"We will face it," Veyrina said, her voice stronger than before. "We've already lost too much. We won't give up now."

The figure's expression remained unreadable, but the faintest flicker of approval passed through its eyes. Without another word, it stepped aside, allowing them to continue forward. The way ahead remained uncertain, but they had made their choice.

As Veyrina and Elyndra moved forward, the echoes grew louder, reverberating through the very core of the realm. They didn't know what awaited them, but one thing was clear: the final trial was coming. And with it, the ultimate test of their love—and of their will to break free.

The path ahead was dark, the air heavy with the scent of impending change. Each step they took felt like a step closer to the unknown, to the end of the cycle that had defined their lives for so long. Would they succeed? Or would the echoes claim them once more?

The silence that followed was filled only by the rhythmic sound of their footsteps, a haunting reminder that the end of their journey was approaching—whether they were ready for it or not.

Nine

The Cost of Remembering

The air shifted as the path ahead grew more intense, the darkness around them palpable, as if the realm itself was holding its breath. Each step that Veyrina and Elyndra took felt heavier, laden with the weight of memories—memories that weren't entirely theirs, but that they carried nonetheless. It was as though the very ground beneath their feet hummed with the resonance of lives they had lived before, lives they had loved and lost.

Veyrina felt her heartbeat quicken, the echoes of those distant lives beginning to pierce her thoughts, threading through her consciousness like a labyrinth of whispers. She staggered, clutching at Elyndra's arm, the weight of the past threatening to crush her. She could hear faint voices, broken fragments of other times—her own voice, Elyndra's, calling out to each other across the chasm of time.

Elyndra's touch, warm and grounding, was the only thing

that kept her from being consumed by the flood. She squeezed Veyrina's hand, her own breath shallow, as if she too was struggling with the onslaught. They were both vulnerable, slipping further into the torrent of their intertwined history.

"Veyrina," Elyndra whispered, her voice strained as if she were reaching out from a place far deeper than the physical realm. "Can you hear them? The echoes… they're so loud. They're all of us, all of them, and it's too much."

Veyrina closed her eyes, trying to steady herself, to breathe through the chaos. But it was no use. The memories, sharp and jagged, were already flooding her mind—each one more intense than the last, each one more crushing.

In one fleeting vision, she saw herself and Elyndra standing on the edge of a cliff in another life. The wind howled around them, the skies swirling in hues of crimson and gold. She remembered the kiss, their final kiss, the one that had torn them apart. In that moment, they had been close to freedom, close to escaping the curse that had bound them. But betrayal had shadowed their steps, a shadow so deep that even their love couldn't outrun it.

Then, the memory shifted. She was in a cold, damp room, the stone walls heavy with age. Elyndra's face was pale, her eyes wide with terror. Veyrina reached out for her, but something unseen, something dark, pulled them apart. The curse was stronger then, the separation final. She had lost Elyndra that day, and the pain was more real than anything she had ever felt before. The walls of her mind trembled, and Veyrina collapsed to her knees, gasping for air, her hands trembling.

"Elyndra…" she whispered through clenched teeth, fighting the overwhelming sensation that was drowning her.

Elyndra dropped to her side, her breath quick and erratic as she held onto Veyrina. "I know. I feel it too," she murmured, her voice shaking with the strain of remembering. "Every time we reach out, the memories pull us back. It's unbearable. It's too much to bear."

Another flood of images hit Veyrina like a tidal wave. She saw them in another life, their love as pure as it had always been, yet doomed by forces they couldn't comprehend. She saw betrayal, secrets whispered in the dark, and the hands of enemies that moved behind the scenes, tightening the chains of the curse that bound them. She saw herself lying, lifeless in Elyndra's arms—again, and again, and again.

The agony in the images overwhelmed her, and she recoiled, shuddering under the weight. She pressed her hands to her temples, her vision swimming. They were trapped, not just by the realm, but by the very essence of the curse itself. The more they tried to escape, the more the memories clawed at them. There was no end, no rest, only the relentless pulse of time, the echo of pain, loss, and unfulfilled promises.

"Stop," Veyrina gasped. "Stop! Please."

Elyndra's voice was raw as she pressed her forehead against Veyrina's, their breaths mingling. "We have to endure this. We have to see it all, or we'll never understand. We can't break the cycle if we can't face what's been done to us."

But Veyrina shook her head, her body trembling as the memories surged again, overwhelming her with each flash of another life. She didn't know how much more she could take—how much longer she could stand before the weight of all the losses destroyed everything they had built. Was their love strong enough to survive this onslaught? Or would the echoes of the past shatter them once and for all?

"Elyndra," Veyrina said, her voice a whisper, fragile as glass.

"Do you think… do you think that love is really worth this? All this suffering? The pain, the separation, the constant breaking?"

Elyndra's grip tightened around her, and she shook her head vehemently. "Yes. I do. I've lived through it all, over and over, and I've never stopped loving you. We've never truly forgotten each other, Veyrina. No matter what we've lost, we've always found our way back. This—this is just another trial. We can't let it destroy us."

Veyrina met Elyndra's gaze, her heart breaking at the depth of her words. How could she deny it? How could she question the love that had persisted through centuries, through the endless cycles of pain? There was a part of her that was terrified—terrified that they would never truly escape, that the curse would consume them entirely. But another part of her, the part that had fought for Elyndra through every lifetime, refused to let go.

"I can't lose you," Veyrina whispered, her voice thick with emotion. "I can't lose us. Not again."

The echoes grew louder, the pulse of time thrumming around them, pressing in from all sides. Veyrina felt herself slipping, the images of their past lives blurring together, each one a painful reminder of what they had endured. But she clung to Elyndra, her heart anchored in the only truth that had ever mattered—her love for her.

Suddenly, the ground beneath them trembled, and the air grew cold, freezing their very breath. A soft voice, ancient and unyielding, whispered through the chaos.

"You are not meant to remember," the voice said. "These memories are not yours to carry. They are chains, binding you to the realm. You cannot break free while you hold onto the past."

Veyrina and Elyndra looked up, their eyes wide, and saw the figure of the Keeper of Echoes standing before them, its form towering and dark. The Keeper's voice was both soothing and terrible, a lullaby laced with poison.

"Let go," the Keeper commanded, its eyes glowing with an intensity that seared into their souls. "Forget. The cost of remembering is too great. Let it all go, and you will be free."

The temptation was there—there in the air between them, pulsing with the promise of relief. The memories, the pain, the fear—they could all fade away, and they could be free of the echoes, free to love without the weight of their past. But at what cost?

Veyrina took a deep breath, her mind racing. The path to freedom was before them, but it was a path she wasn't sure she could walk. Could she forget the love they had shared? Could she erase the depth of her connection to Elyndra?

"No," she said firmly, shaking her head. "We can't forget. Not again."

Elyndra's voice was equally strong as she held Veyrina's gaze. "We've already lived through the cost of forgetting. We'll fight through this, together. We've endured too much to let go now."

The Keeper's eyes flickered, as though searching for weakness, but it did not speak again. For a long moment, the world held its breath, the echoes of their past lives fading into a heavy silence.

In the stillness, Veyrina and Elyndra stood united, their hands entwined, their hearts steadfast. They would not forget. No matter the cost, they would face the pain, the memories, and the echoes. They would break the cycle—not by erasing their past, but by accepting it, and by enduring it together.

And in that moment, as the echoes began to fade, Veyrina realized that the true cost of remembering wasn't in the weight of the past—it was in the strength to continue loving through it all.

The weight of their decision hung in the air, pressing down like the oppressive stillness of the deep night. The echoes around them softened, as if the realm itself was watching, waiting to see if they would truly defy the Keeper's offer.

Veyrina's grip on Elyndra's hand tightened, her pulse quickening as a shudder ran through her. She had made her choice. She had chosen the pain, the memories, and the love that lived beneath them all. But the question still lingered: Was it enough to break the cycle? Could their love, battered by time and betrayal, truly withstand the forces at work in this cursed realm?

The Keeper stood motionless, its glowing eyes studying them with a kind of patience that was both unsettling and impenetrable. Its voice echoed again, this time quieter, almost a whisper.

"You have chosen," the Keeper intoned, its tone neither kind nor cruel, simply indifferent. "But do you understand what it means? The past will never release its grip on you. And love… love will cost you more than you can imagine."

Veyrina's heart pounded as she felt the echoes surge again, stronger this time, more insistent. The images from their past lives—the betrayals, the painful goodbyes, the moments of love they had shared—flashed before her eyes in rapid succession. The overwhelming weight of it all felt like drowning, like the floodgates had opened and the force of everything they had been, and everything they had lost, was pouring through her.

Elyndra seemed to be struggling as well. She swayed, her face pale, and Veyrina could feel the tremors in her hand. She was fighting the pull of the memories too. They had both known this moment would come—the moment where their love would be tested, where the echoes of their past would demand their sacrifice. And now, it seemed they were being asked to face the ultimate question: Would they be able to withstand the pressure, or would the weight of the past break them apart forever?

"Elyndra," Veyrina whispered, her voice cracking. "Can you hear it? The echoes… they're louder than before. They're so close to swallowing us whole."

Elyndra's breath hitched, her eyes wide with fear. But there was also a flicker of something else in her gaze. A determination, perhaps? A longing to protect their bond, to shield it from the past that had constantly tried to tear it apart.

"I hear them," Elyndra replied softly, her voice breaking through the chaos of memories that swirled around them. "But we have to keep going, Veyrina. We have to keep pushing through. We've survived this long—together. We can't stop now."

Tears welled in Veyrina's eyes as the memories crashed against her like a relentless tide. But she held onto Elyndra, as if her touch was the only lifeline between her and the abyss.

"I don't know if I can take much more of this," Veyrina whispered, her voice tight with emotion. "The memories are too much. The pain… the loss… it's all so overwhelming."

Elyndra's expression softened, and she gently cupped Veyrina's face, her fingers warm against the cool skin of Veyrina's cheek. The moment was tender, even amidst the turmoil, and it grounded Veyrina in a way she hadn't realized she needed.

Elyndra's eyes searched hers, deep and unwavering.

"You're not alone," Elyndra said, her voice steady, full of the strength Veyrina had come to rely on. "We've been through this before. We've endured it together. We can do it again. We will do it again. Our love is stronger than the echoes, Veyrina. It always has been."

For a long moment, they stood there, staring into each other's eyes, the world around them fading as the truth of Elyndra's words settled into Veyrina's soul. The echoes would not be silent. They would never fully disappear, and the pain of their past lives would always be a part of them. But Veyrina realized, in that instant, that it didn't matter.

The love they shared was far greater than the curse that had bound them. The memories, as painful as they were, didn't define them. It was the love between them that mattered— the love that had endured for lifetimes, the love that would continue to fight through the darkness.

Suddenly, the air around them shifted again, colder this time. A chill ran down Veyrina's spine, and the shadows in the realm seemed to grow darker, as if responding to the choices they had made. The Keeper's voice rang out, now heavy with an unsettling edge.

"You think you can defy the cycle," the Keeper's voice echoed, its tone a deep, resonating threat. "But you cannot escape the truth. Love is not enough. It never has been. You will suffer, and you will lose. In the end, the echoes will consume you."

But Veyrina and Elyndra stood firm, their hands still entwined, their gazes locked with unwavering resolve.

"No," Veyrina said, her voice steady now, stronger than she had ever felt before. "Love is enough. It has always been enough. And no matter what happens, we will face it together."

Elyndra nodded, her expression resolute. "We've already endured the worst of the past. Whatever the Keeper throws at us, we'll face it—together."

The Keeper's eyes narrowed, its gaze piercing into them with an intensity that made Veyrina's skin prickle. But it said nothing further, merely watching them with an unreadable expression.

The air around them shimmered, a strange force swirling as if the realm itself were reacting to their defiance. The echoes, once deafening, began to quiet, retreating into the distance like a fading storm. The pressure, the suffocating weight of the memories, began to lift, slowly but surely. And for the first time, Veyrina felt a sliver of hope—a fragile thread of light cutting through the darkness.

"We're not done yet," Elyndra whispered, a smile breaking through the tension, though her eyes remained wary. "But we've made it this far. Together."

Veyrina smiled back, her heart swelling with the warmth of their shared resolve. No matter what came next, they would face it side by side, refusing to let the curse tear them apart. The echoes may still call to them, but they had reclaimed their love. And that, Veyrina realized, was the truest victory of all.

But just as they began to feel the first stirrings of relief, a sudden, jarring noise pierced the silence. A low, guttural sound, like the growl of some great beast from the depths of the realm. The Keeper's eyes flared with a dangerous gleam, and the air around them turned ice-cold.

"You have not won," the Keeper's voice rumbled, more menacing now. "The cost of remembering is not just your past. It is your future. And I will see to it that you pay."

Before Veyrina and Elyndra could react, the ground beneath

them began to tremble once more, and the echoes rose louder than ever, filling the space with a cacophony of sound—a thousand voices calling, demanding, threatening.

The battle was far from over.

Ten

The Wraith's Curse

The air was thick with an otherworldly chill, a shiver of unseen forces threading through the shadows of the echo realm. Veyrina and Elyndra stood at the threshold of the ancient stone circle, their eyes drawn to the fog that curled around their feet, swirling like the whispers of the past. The echoes were louder now, more insistent, vibrating within them like an unrelenting pulse.

"We must keep moving," Veyrina said, her voice barely above a whisper. She could feel it, the impending danger, a weight in the very air that pressed down on her chest. Her fingers, trembling, clutched the amulet that hung around her neck, a talisman forged from the remnants of an old relic—one that, until now, had been their only source of protection.

Elyndra turned to her, her face etched with a mixture of determination and apprehension. The battle they'd fought against the shifting echoes, against the crumbling remnants of their shared memories, had not been easy. But this… this felt different. The air crackled with something darker, more threatening.

"It's not just the echoes anymore," Elyndra murmured, her eyes scanning the fog, her senses stretched thin. "Something else is here. Something we can't control."

Veyrina nodded, knowing exactly what Elyndra meant. The realm had shifted, and the subtle tension that had once felt like an unfathomable mystery now began to take shape. The air was no longer simply thick with time—it was thick with malice.

They had been tracking the echoes for what felt like an eternity, each step drawing them closer to the center of the realm, where the answers they sought lay hidden. But now, something had changed. The whispers were louder, more oppressive. And the shadows that stretched long across the land seemed to pulse with an ancient hunger.

It was then that they heard it.

A low, guttural sound, like the rustling of dry leaves, except it was much too deliberate, much too human. Veyrina's breath caught in her throat, and Elyndra instinctively stepped closer, her hand brushing Veyrina's as if to reassure them both that they were still together, still tethered by something stronger than fear.

Then, from the fog, a figure emerged.

Tall, impossibly tall, draped in robes that seemed to blend with the darkness itself. The figure's face was obscured by a hood, but there was no mistaking the ominous presence that radiated from it. The wraith.

It stood silently for a moment, its ethereal form flickering in and out of existence like a reflection in shattered glass.

And then, its voice—a voice that sounded both distant and immediate, like a distant echo reverberating through time— spoke.

"You cannot escape," the wraith intoned, its voice carrying an unnatural weight, as though the words had been spoken across centuries. "Your love is cursed. Bound to this realm forever. And you will be torn apart, just as you were before."

Veyrina felt a shiver crawl up her spine, her heart pounding in her chest. She knew that voice. It wasn't just the wraith's— it was a voice that had spoken to her before, in dreams, in moments where the echoes of the past had bled into her present. This was no mere being. It was an agent of the curse, a creature forged by the very forces that had trapped them in this endless cycle.

Elyndra's jaw tightened, her eyes narrowing as she regarded the wraith with a mixture of defiance and dread. "We've broken free of your games before," she said, her voice steady despite the fear that gnawed at the edges of her words. "We'll do it again."

The wraith chuckled, a hollow, rasping sound that sent a chill through the air. "You think you've escaped," it said, stepping forward, the shadows gathering around it like a cloak. "But you've only deluded yourselves. The echoes grow stronger, and your bond… it weakens with each cycle. You will never break free. And now… you will pay the price for your defiance."

The wraith extended a hand, a dark tendril of shadow snaking from its fingers and wrapping around the stone beneath their feet. Veyrina flinched, her breath catching as the ground seemed to tremble beneath her. The wraith was feeding on the echoes now, pulling the energy from the very essence of their love, using it to grow stronger.

Elyndra stepped forward, her eyes locked on the wraith with a fierce intensity. "We won't let you have us," she said, the words coming out sharper now, tinged with a deep, unshakable conviction. "We'll destroy you, no matter what it takes."

The wraith's laugh was soft, almost mocking. "You don't understand, child. It is not you who will destroy me. It is you who will destroy yourselves." It turned its gaze toward Veyrina, and the room seemed to pulse with the dark energy that emanated from it. "You, too, are bound to the curse. And the more you fight against it, the more it will devour you."

Veyrina's stomach twisted. She could feel the pull of the wraith, the crushing weight of its power pressing against her chest. She struggled to breathe, to keep her footing as the ground beneath her began to shift, as though the realm itself was bending to the wraith's will.

"You have one choice," the wraith continued, its voice a low, insidious hum. "Surrender, or sacrifice one for the other. One must die for the other to live. It is the only way to break the curse."

Veyrina's heart stuttered in her chest, and she turned to Elyndra, her eyes wide with horror. "No," she whispered, barely able to force the words past the lump in her throat. "We can't—"

Elyndra's hand gripped hers, strong and sure despite the fear that tightened her features. "We won't choose that. There's always another way."

The wraith's cold eyes glinted, a flicker of something cruel dancing within them. "Then you will fail," it said, its form beginning to dissolve into the shadows. "The curse will consume you both. And in the end, you will be nothing but echoes—trapped, forgotten, and alone."

As the wraith vanished, the air grew still, the oppressive weight of its presence lifting slightly, though the threat lingered, hanging in the air like a storm ready to break.

Veyrina turned to Elyndra, her heart pounding as the echoes of their past swirled around them, a reminder of everything they stood to lose. "What now?" she asked, her voice barely a whisper.

Elyndra swallowed hard, her hand still clutching Veyrina's. She didn't have an answer. Not yet. But the decision loomed large, and they both knew that the wraith's curse was not a choice they could ignore for long.

"We fight," Elyndra said, her voice firm with resolve. "We fight, and we find a way to break this—together."

But as the last of the wraith's dark presence faded into the distance, the two of them knew, deep down, that this battle would demand more than either of them had ever imagined. The curse was not just a force—they were its chosen victims, bound by fate, cursed by love, and torn apart by the very echoes they had fought to remember. And now, they would have to face the cost of remembering, and of the choices they had yet to make.

The silence after the wraith's departure hung like a fog, thick and stifling. For a moment, Veyrina and Elyndra stood in the swirling mist, the weight of the wraith's words pressing on them, pulling them deeper into the darkness of the realm.

Veyrina's mind raced, a whirlwind of thoughts clashing against one another. The wraith's prophecy—its offer of sacrifice—repeated over and over in her mind. *One must die for the other to live.* She couldn't fathom the truth of it. Could they really be forced into such a decision? Could they truly sacrifice one another? She couldn't stand the thought of it. The bond they shared was the one thing that had kept her going through countless lifetimes. To sever it would feel like losing her very soul.

But Elyndra's grip on her hand remained strong, warm even in the cold of the echo realm. Veyrina looked into her eyes, searching for the certainty, the unshakable trust that had always been there. She could see the flickers of fear and doubt in Elyndra's eyes, but there was something else, too. A quiet resolve.

"We have to destroy it," Elyndra whispered, breaking the silence between them. Her voice was steady, but there was a fire in her eyes that Veyrina hadn't seen before. "We can't give in to what the wraith wants. We can't give in to this curse."

Veyrina nodded, her heart swelling with both fear and determination. She had known from the start that their journey wouldn't be easy. But this—this was more than they could have ever anticipated.

"How?" Veyrina asked, her voice trembling despite the resolve she was trying to muster. "We can't even begin to understand what we're dealing with. The wraith feeds on our love, Elyndra. How do we destroy something that is tied to us so deeply?"

Elyndra's jaw tightened, her gaze unwavering as she stepped closer, her forehead pressing gently against Veyrina's. "We find its source," she said softly. "We find the heart of the curse, the root of this magic, and we tear it apart. We've done it before, and we will do it again."

Veyrina closed her eyes for a moment, allowing herself to take in Elyndra's words. The past had given them more than one lesson in resilience, in the strength of their connection.

They had overcome so many trials together, so many losses. But the thought of a battle this grand—this personal—struck a chord of fear within her. It wasn't just about surviving the curse anymore. It was about confronting the deepest darkness within themselves.

"We need to find out where the curse began," Veyrina said, her mind already racing with possibilities. "We need to trace the magic back to its origin. The wraith... it was born from that same magic. It must know something about where the curse lies."

Elyndra nodded, her lips pressing into a thin line. "We'll find it. But we can't let the wraith know our plans. It's too powerful. If it senses even the smallest crack in our resolve, it will tear us apart."

Veyrina's fingers tightened around Elyndra's, her heart pounding with the weight of the decision that loomed ahead. They were running out of time. The echoes were growing louder again, swelling around them like an invisible tide, pulling them into the current of their past lives.

Suddenly, a sharp, eerie cry split the air—too close, too familiar. Veyrina froze, her heart leaping in her chest.

The wraith. It had returned.

With a quick glance at Elyndra, they both knew what they had to do. There was no time to waste. They had to move fast, or the wraith's influence would consume them both. The shadows thickened, and the ground beneath their feet seemed to shift, becoming more unstable with each passing moment.

The wraith's figure materialized from the fog again, its form shimmering like a mirage. Its face remained hidden beneath the hood, but Veyrina could feel its gaze upon them, cold and unyielding.

"You cannot escape," the wraith intoned, its voice ringing with a chilling finality. "The cycle is already set in motion. The past cannot be undone. And neither can you."

Veyrina stood tall, defiance rising in her chest. "We'll see about that," she said, her voice filled with unwavering conviction.

With one last glance at Elyndra, Veyrina stepped forward, her hand reaching into the folds of her cloak. She could feel the weight of the amulet against her chest, the one object that had sustained them both through the most desperate of times. It was no longer just a symbol of their love; it was their weapon, their key to breaking free from the chains that bound them.

As she clasped the amulet tightly, a surge of energy pulsed through her. The air crackled, and the shadows recoiled, as if the very realm itself was aware of their intent. The wraith's laughter, hollow and cruel, echoed through the mist.

"You think you can defeat me?" the wraith taunted, its voice reverberating like a thousand whispers at once. "Your love is nothing more than a curse. It will always return, always bind you. You cannot escape what is written."

Veyrina's pulse quickened, her grip on the amulet tightening. "We'll write our own ending," she said, her voice laced with raw power.

And with that, she raised the amulet high, letting its energy flare outward. The shadows recoiled as a burst of brilliant light erupted from the amulet, illuminating the darkness like a beacon.

The wraith howled, its form flickering as if it were struggling against the light. The air thickened with tension, the space between Veyrina, Elyndra, and the wraith collapsing into a charged battlefield. Veyrina could feel the energy from the amulet flowing through her, building, strengthening with each heartbeat.

"Together," Elyndra whispered fiercely, stepping beside her. Her hand gripped Veyrina's, a silent promise to stand side by side no matter what came.

The wraith shrieked, a piercing, agonized sound that vibrated through Veyrina's very bones. The light from the amulet flickered, casting jagged shadows as it struggled against the wraith's growing power.

"Let go of your love," the wraith hissed, its form shifting in a frantic attempt to break free. "Let go, and you may survive. Hold on, and you will be consumed."

For a heartbeat, the air around them seemed to stop, the world holding its breath.

Veyrina looked into Elyndra's eyes, and in that moment, she knew. Their love was not just a force of nature—it was their strength. The wraith could not take it from them. They had endured this before, and they would endure it again.

With one final surge of energy, Veyrina and Elyndra both pressed the amulet forward, channeling their shared will into a single, blinding pulse of light.

The wraith screamed in agony, its form disintegrating into nothingness, the shadows fleeing before the blinding brilliance. The very air seemed to tremble as the light reached its peak, engulfing the realm in a dazzling flare that left nothing but silence in its wake.

When the light faded, the wraith was gone.

But the price had been paid.

Veyrina and Elyndra stood, their bodies trembling from the effort, their hearts heavy with the knowledge that their fight was far from over. The echoes remained, but they had struck a blow against the curse, one that would leave its mark forever. They were not free yet, but they had taken the first step. And together, they would face whatever came next.

Eleven

The Light Beyond the Echo

The air in the echo realm grew still, as if holding its breath. Veyrina and Elyndra stood at the edge of a cliff, their eyes locked on the horizon. Before them, the realm stretched out endlessly—shifting landscapes that bled into one another, too fluid to define. The wind, though soft, carried a charge, crackling like static, as if the world itself was on the brink of change.

It was Elyndra who first saw it—a faint shimmer in the air, like a veil pulled across the fabric of reality. A portal, half-hidden by the fog of the realm, glowed with an ethereal light. The sight of it caused a strange stirring in Veyrina's chest, a mix of hope and dread.

"What is that?" Elyndra's voice was barely a whisper, as though speaking too loudly might shatter the fragile illusion.

"I don't know," Veyrina replied, her pulse quickening. "But it feels… important."

They had been searching for a way out of the echo for so long that the idea of finally finding an exit seemed almost too good to be true. Veyrina stepped forward, her eyes fixed on the glowing gateway, feeling an undeniable pull toward it. She could sense the weight of the choice hanging in the air—what lay beyond might be their salvation, or it could lead them deeper into the labyrinth of their torment.

Elyndra hesitated, her hand brushing against Veyrina's arm as if for reassurance. There was a question in her gaze, unspoken but heavy in its silence. *Do we dare?*

Veyrina felt her heart tighten at the question, the uncertainty in Elyndra's eyes mirroring her own. The portal shimmered, flickering like a flame caught in the wind, and then, as if sensing their indecision, it began to pulse with brighter light, urging them forward.

"Do you feel that?" Elyndra asked, her voice trembling.

Veyrina nodded. "Yes."

It was as though the very essence of the realm had changed, the air thick with a strange kind of tension, something ancient and far-reaching. There was no turning back. They both knew it, and yet, neither could fully embrace the choice. A lifetime of doubts, insecurities, and fears loomed between them, and they had only each other to rely on.

"I think it's time," Veyrina murmured. "We've come this far together. If we're going to be free, we have to trust each other."

Elyndra turned to her, her eyes dark with unspoken emotion. For a moment, it felt as though time stood still. Veyrina's heart pounded in her chest, the weight of the moment nearly suffocating. The connection between them had always been deep—so deep that it felt like a tether, pulling them together no matter how much they fought against it. But this… this felt different. There was something in Elyndra's gaze that spoke of hesitation, something buried beneath the surface of their bond.

Elyndra nodded, her lips curling into a faint, bittersweet smile. "Then let's go."

Together, they stepped toward the portal, their hands brushing against each other, their fingers intertwining. The light grew brighter, consuming them in its glow, and the world around them began to fade. It was as if they were being drawn into the very heart of the echo—no longer just part of it, but rather the focal point of its existence. The realm around them seemed to contract, folding inward like the petals of a flower, until there was nothing but light and shadow.

The moment they crossed the threshold, they were enveloped in a wave of energy. A cold, biting wind tore through them, raking across their skin like icy fingers. The world around them spun, disorienting and surreal, as though they were trapped between realms, neither here nor there.

Elyndra gasped, her body shuddering with the force of the transition. Veyrina's heart raced, her breath coming in quick, shallow bursts as she struggled to find her bearings. She turned to Elyndra, her face pale, but her eyes burning with determination. *We can do this. We have to.*

But then, the portal closed behind them with a deafening roar, and the world around them solidified. They found themselves standing in a vast chamber, its walls made of stone that seemed to pulse with an ancient energy. The ceiling arched high above them, far beyond their sight, and the air was thick with an oppressive silence that made their hearts beat louder.

And in the center of the room, standing tall and still as a statue, was the figure of a woman—the Keeper.

Her presence was overwhelming. She was neither fully here nor there, as if her very being existed in multiple places at once, straddling the boundaries of the realms. Her eyes glowed with an eerie, otherworldly light, and her hands were clasped in front of her, her fingers twisted in a gesture of power.

"You have come," the Keeper's voice echoed through the chamber, low and resonant, filling every corner with its presence. It was not just a voice—they could feel it deep in their bones, vibrating through the very marrow of their existence.

Veyrina's heart skipped a beat. "Who are you?"

"I am the Keeper of Echoes," the woman replied, her gaze shifting between them, never settling for too long on either of them. "The one who holds the keys to the past and the future, to the memories and the loss that bind you."

Elyndra took a step forward, her voice steady but trembling with a mixture of awe and fear. "What do you want from us?"

The Keeper tilted her head slightly, as though considering the question. "I offer you a choice," she said, her voice smooth as silk. "A choice that will shape your destiny."

The words hung heavy in the air, like a storm waiting to break. Veyrina's eyes narrowed as she watched the Keeper closely, every instinct telling her that there was more to this than she could see.

"What choice?" Elyndra asked, her voice tinged with both hope and suspicion.

"You have the power to escape the echo," the Keeper intoned. "But in doing so, you must give up the very thing that brought you here—the bond between you. You may walk away, free of the curse, free of the realm. Or you may remain, and risk everything—your love, your memories, your very existence—fighting against the forces that bind you."

A silence fell between them as the weight of the Keeper's words sank in. The choice was simple, yet impossibly complex. Freedom at the cost of their love… or endless struggle for a love that might never be theirs to claim.

Veyrina's chest tightened. The thought of losing Elyndra, of walking away from the bond that had drawn them together through lifetimes, was unbearable. But at the same time, the idea of continuing to fight, to remain trapped in the cycle of echoes, seemed just as unbearable.

The Keeper stepped forward, her eyes gleaming with the knowledge of their deepest fears. "You must decide. The trial will test you—test your love, your resolve, and your willingness to sacrifice. Only then will you know if the light beyond the echo is worth the price."

Veyrina felt a shiver run through her as the Keeper's words lingered in the air, pressing down on them like a physical weight. She turned to Elyndra, her heart heavy with uncertainty.

"What do we do?" Elyndra whispered, her voice barely audible.

Veyrina took a deep breath, her hand finding Elyndra's, fingers trembling as she squeezed. "We face it. Together."

And with that, they took their first step into the unknown, toward the trial that would determine the fate of their love and the future they would share—or not share—forever.

But the road ahead was shrouded in darkness, and the echo still lingered, pulsing with the promise of what could be.

Veyrina and Elyndra stood before the Keeper, the weight of her presence pressing down on them like a thousand invisible hands. The chamber was vast, and yet it felt constricting, as though the walls were slowly closing in with each passing moment. The Keeper's eyes glimmered with the knowledge of countless lifetimes, and her voice echoed in the chamber like the reverberation of a bell tolling in a distant place.

"Are you ready to face the trial?" the Keeper asked, her voice low, almost a whisper, but one that resonated with power.

Veyrina felt her heart hammering in her chest. The Keeper's words hung in the air like a question without an answer, an invitation into the unknown. She turned to Elyndra, searching her face for some semblance of clarity, but she saw only the same uncertainty mirrored in Elyndra's eyes.

"Are we ready?" Elyndra echoed, her voice uncertain, but her grip on Veyrina's hand tight and resolute.

"I don't know," Veyrina admitted softly, her voice breaking the silence between them. "But we can't turn back now."

The Keeper watched them with an almost calculating intensity, as though measuring their every thought, every hesitation. She tilted her head slightly, then spoke again, her voice laced with a strange, almost sadistic amusement.

"The trial awaits," she said. "But know this—only by embracing your deepest fears, by confronting the doubts that cloud your bond, will you find the truth of your love. Your connection will be tested, strained until it is pushed to its breaking point. What remains after that will be the answer you seek."

Veyrina swallowed hard, her throat dry. The Keeper's words had the bite of truth to them, though she wasn't sure whether they were meant to encourage or torment. The trial was not a test of strength, nor of their will to escape. It was a test of their love. A test of whether they could truly break free from the echoes of their past, or if they were destined to be bound forever to this endless cycle of longing and separation.

The Keeper raised a hand, and the air around them began to shimmer with a strange, silvery light. The ground trembled beneath their feet, and the world around them seemed to distort, warping and bending in on itself. Veyrina's stomach lurched as a deep sense of vertigo swept over her. She gripped Elyndra's hand tighter, and the two of them were drawn forward, as though an unseen force was guiding them into the unknown.

They walked together, each step heavy, their hearts beating in unison. As they approached the center of the chamber, the air thickened, becoming suffocating. The temperature dropped, and Veyrina could see her breath fogging in front of her. She glanced around, trying to make sense of what was happening, but the space around them seemed to stretch and contract, twisting like a dream caught between worlds.

And then, just as the pressure became unbearable, the world around them fractured.

With a snap of light and sound, they were plunged into darkness.

Veyrina gasped, her hand reaching out blindly for Elyndra's. But there was no warmth, no solid ground beneath her feet. She was falling, tumbling through a void that seemed to stretch out forever. The sensation was disorienting, terrifying—an endless descent into something unknown.

She felt a hand catch hers, a firm grip pulling her back, grounding her in the swirling abyss. Elyndra's voice, strained with panic, reached her ears.

"Veyrina! Where are you?"

"I'm here!" Veyrina cried out, her voice trembling as she reached blindly in the darkness. "Elyndra, I'm here!"

The grip on her hand tightened, and she could feel Elyndra's presence, her warmth, even in the darkness. They weren't alone. They never were. Their bond was the only constant, the only thing they could trust in this chaos.

Suddenly, the darkness began to dissolve, replaced by a dim, flickering light. It was not the soft, welcoming glow of the portal they had crossed through—it was harsh, sharp, and filled with a sinister undercurrent. The light cast long shadows on the walls, twisting and contorting into shapes that made Veyrina's skin crawl.

They were standing now, not in the chamber they had left behind, but in a cold, desolate wasteland. The ground beneath them was cracked and barren, the earth a dark, ashen gray. The sky above was a sickly green, swirling with clouds that seemed to move with a life of their own.

A voice echoed across the desolation, low and mocking.

"Welcome to the trial," it said. The voice was distorted, as though it was coming from every direction at once, and yet it felt strangely familiar. It sent a chill down Veyrina's spine.

"Who's there?" Elyndra demanded, her voice fierce, but Veyrina could hear the tremor of uncertainty beneath the surface. She gripped Elyndra's hand harder, the connection between them a lifeline in this forsaken place.

From the shadows, a figure emerged. Tall and cloaked in tattered robes, its face obscured by a hood. The figure moved with unsettling grace, its footsteps silent as it approached them. Veyrina felt an overwhelming sense of foreboding wash over her, but she forced herself to stand tall. They couldn't afford to falter now.

"You are here to face yourselves," the figure said, its voice a strange blend of warmth and venom. "To confront the doubts that have held you captive for countless lifetimes. Only when you have faced the truth will you be able to move beyond the echo."

Veyrina and Elyndra exchanged a glance, and Veyrina saw the same fear reflected in Elyndra's eyes that she felt burning in her own chest. This was the moment—the moment they would have to face the heart of their fears.

The figure raised a hand, and suddenly, the ground beneath them seemed to shift. The air shimmered again, and before Veyrina could react, she was no longer standing in the wasteland.

Instead, she was in a room—small, dimly lit, and eerily familiar.

The walls were lined with portraits, each one depicting a woman she knew well, a woman whose name she had long forgotten.

It was Elyndra.

Elyndra, but not the Elyndra standing beside her now. This Elyndra was cold, distant, her eyes hollow with sorrow. She was trapped in the frame of each painting, her face a mask of anguish.

"Do you see it?" the voice of the figure whispered from the shadows. "This is who you've been to her. This is the face of your love—the face you have forgotten, the face you can never truly escape."

Veyrina stumbled back, her breath catching in her throat. The paintings around her blurred and shifted, the faces twisting into something grotesque and alien. Each one seemed to mock her, to whisper of all the pain they had endured.

And then, a whisper reached her ear.

"You've failed her, Veyrina. Over and over. How many

lifetimes have you forgotten her? How many times have you abandoned her for your own selfish desires?"

Veyrina's chest tightened, and the weight of the accusation pressed down on her. Was it true? Had she truly abandoned Elyndra, over and over again?

She turned to Elyndra, who stood beside her, but the look in Elyndra's eyes was no longer one of unwavering love. There was doubt there—doubt in her, in their connection.

"Elyndra…" Veyrina whispered, her voice breaking. "I—"

But Elyndra took a step back, her face turning away.

"How can I trust you, Veyrina?" Elyndra's voice was barely audible. "How can I trust you when I've been left alone so many times before?"

The pain in Elyndra's words struck like a blade to the heart, and Veyrina's knees buckled beneath her. The room around her seemed to collapse inward, suffocating her with the weight of her own failures.

"Trust… trust…" Veyrina gasped. "I—I never meant to hurt you."

But the echo of Elyndra's words lingered, louder and louder, until they drowned out everything else.

"Are you truly willing to face the consequences of your love?" the voice of the Keeper echoed in the space. "Or are you doomed to repeat the cycle forever?"

Veyrina could barely hear it over the storm of her own doubts. This was the trial—the test of their bond.

The Unseen Realm

The moment they crossed the threshold of the portal, everything changed.

A violent shudder ran through Veyrina's bones as the world around them dissolved into a blur of shifting colors. It felt as though they were being pulled apart, their very essence scattered across a vast and unending expanse. The weight of the echo realm, the suffocating grasp of the cycle they had tried to escape, lifted for a heartbeat. But it was quickly replaced by an overwhelming sense of vertigo—something more profound, something older, far more ancient than anything they had encountered.

Then, with a sudden, jarring thud, the sensation of weightlessness vanished. The air shifted, thickening with a strange, acrid scent. The ground beneath them was solid—too solid. It felt unnatural, as though the world itself had rejected them, allowing them only brief respite before snapping them back into the reality of their eternal struggle.

Veyrina stumbled forward, her hands outstretched, her fingers grazing the coarse, cracked earth beneath her feet. Her heart pounded in her chest as she struggled to breathe, the air dense and stifling, as though the very atmosphere was filled with the weight of unspoken history.

Elyndra's hand gripped hers with a surprising force, the warmth of her touch anchoring Veyrina to the present moment. "Where are we?" Elyndra's voice was a quiet whisper, but Veyrina could hear the tremor of uncertainty in her words. Even Elyndra, so steadfast, felt the pull of this unknown place.

"I don't know," Veyrina replied, her voice steady despite the fear clawing at her chest. "But we're not in the echo anymore. This place… it feels different."

The world around them was a twisted reflection of what they had known. Above them, the sky raged with fire, bleeding into shades of crimson and violet as if the heavens themselves were burning. Below their feet, the earth was cracked and dry, its surface a patchwork of jagged rocks and scorched sand. The landscape stretched endlessly in every direction—there were no boundaries, no borders to this strange world. A vast expanse of chaos, a mixture of frozen seas, burning skies, and endless deserts that seemed to pulse with a dissonant energy.

"This isn't right," Elyndra muttered, her voice barely audible above the unnerving silence. "This place… it's wrong."

Veyrina could only nod in agreement. The very air felt charged, thick with something they couldn't name. A pressure hung in the atmosphere like the moment before a storm, and she knew, with an unsettling certainty, that this place wasn't just a new realm—it was a prison. A prison unlike any they had ever known.

Suddenly, a sound cut through the silence—a low, melodic hum that seemed to vibrate through the very ground beneath them. The air shimmered, distorting with the force of an unseen power. Veyrina's heart skipped a beat as a figure appeared before them, materializing from the very fabric of the chaos itself.

The figure was tall, cloaked in dark, tattered robes, with eyes that gleamed like polished obsidian. Her features were sharp, almost regal, and yet there was an unsettling aura about her, as though her presence alone could bend the world to her will.

Veyrina instinctively took a step back, her fingers tightening around Elyndra's hand. The stranger's gaze shifted to them, her eyes narrowing in recognition, before a cold smile stretched across her lips.

"Veyrina," the woman said, her voice smooth, almost musical, yet laced with an edge that sent a shiver down Veyrina's spine. "I see you've found your way here."

Elyndra stiffened beside her, her grip tightening on Veyrina's hand as she too took in the woman's appearance. There was a flicker of recognition in Elyndra's eyes, quickly masked by a veil of indifference.

"Maelithra," Elyndra said, her voice tinged with a mix of wariness and reluctance. "What are you doing here?"

The woman—Maelithra—tilted her head slightly, her dark eyes flickering with something like amusement. "You never were good at letting go of the past, were you, Elyndra?" she said softly, her words dripping with a kind of bittersweet nostalgia. "I see you still carry the weight of our shared memories."

Elyndra's face tightened, her jaw clenching as though the mention of Maelithra's name was a wound she could never quite heal. Veyrina could feel the tension radiating off Elyndra, the unspoken history between them crackling in the air like an electric current.

"What do you want, Maelithra?" Elyndra asked, her voice low and controlled, but there was an edge to it now—a defensive sharpness that Veyrina had never heard before.

Maelithra's smile softened, a sadness in her gaze as she looked between the two women. "I'm here because I have a message for you both," she said, her voice suddenly heavy with gravity. "You've crossed into the Unseen Realm, a place that lies outside of the rules you know. It is not a place meant for the living—or the dead, for that matter. Here, time does not flow as it should. Here, there are no certainties. The past, the present, the future—they are all intertwined in ways that cannot be understood."

Elyndra took a step forward, her eyes narrowing. "You're not making any sense."

Maelithra's expression hardened, the sadness in her eyes turning to something darker, more dangerous. "The truth is this: The echoes you've been running from, the cycles of separation that bind you, are not the only forces at play in your fate. The cost of your freedom—if you truly wish to break free of the echoes—is not one that can be paid lightly. There are forces beyond this realm that would see you remain trapped here, forever."

Veyrina's pulse quickened, her breath hitching in her throat. "What are you talking about?" she demanded. "What forces? And why are you here?"

Maelithra met her gaze directly, her eyes dark and heavy with secrets. "I was once a part of this world—of Elyndra's life—but now I am bound to this place. I seek redemption for what I have done, for the choices I made that led me here. The same choices you two are about to face."

Elyndra's eyes flashed with confusion and something else—pain. "You're telling me that your redemption is tied to us? That we have to help you?"

Maelithra's smile was bitter, a wisp of a laugh escaping her lips. "Not help. Only understand. I can't undo what I've done. But perhaps you can. There are truths in this realm that can unravel the threads of fate you've been trying to escape. But they come at a cost, one that might tear your bond apart."

Veyrina felt her throat tighten. "What cost? What do you want from us?"

Maelithra's eyes flickered with an emotion that Veyrina couldn't place—something raw, something desperate. "Your love," she whispered. "You will have to give it up, to sever your connection. One of you must choose to leave the other behind, or the cycle will never end. It is the only way to break the curse of this place."

Elyndra's face went pale, her expression one of pure disbelief. "No," she breathed, her voice trembling. "You can't ask that of us. We've already lost so much… You can't make us—"

Maelithra raised a hand, silencing her. "You already know the price, Elyndra. Don't you?" Her voice was soft, almost tender. "This place, this realm—it feeds on your love, on the power of the bond you share. If you want to leave, if you want to break free, one of you must walk away. It is the only way."

The silence stretched between them, thick and suffocating. Veyrina's mind raced, her heart thundering in her chest as she processed Maelithra's words. The world around them seemed to tilt, the edges of reality warping as the weight of the decision hung in the air.

"One of us… must leave?" Elyndra's voice cracked, the pain

in her words unmistakable.

Maelithra nodded slowly. "Yes. Only then will you be free. The choice is yours."

Veyrina glanced at Elyndra, her heart breaking with the weight of the decision before them. They had fought so hard to be together, to break free of the echoes that bound them. But now, the very thing they had fought for—their love—was the one thing that could keep them trapped.

And as they stood in the Unseen Realm, the truth hit Veyrina like a thunderclap.

The cost of freedom was far higher than either of them had ever imagined.

The weight of Maelithra's words hung in the air, suffocating and unyielding. Veyrina could feel her pulse pounding in her ears, the enormity of what she was hearing crashing over her like a storm. She looked at Elyndra, her heart aching with the thought of what was being asked of them.

Elyndra's face had drained of color. She stood frozen, her hands trembling at her sides, but her gaze was locked on Maelithra as if trying to understand if this was some cruel joke. The very idea of choosing to sever their bond—of leaving each other behind—was unfathomable.

"I—I don't understand," Elyndra stammered, her voice barely above a whisper. "Why do we have to sacrifice our love? How does that even make sense? We've fought so hard to get this far. Why now?"

Maelithra's expression softened, though there was no warmth in it. "The bond you share is the reason you're here. It is the reason you've been trapped in the echo realm, over and over again. Your love, your connection—it is what binds you to this place. It gives the Unseen Realm its power. It is the very thing that both keeps you trapped and can free you."

Veyrina's chest tightened. The implications of Maelithra's words were becoming clearer, and with each passing second, the suffocating weight of their situation grew heavier. The bond they had fought so fiercely to preserve—could it really be the thing that kept them bound here forever?

"Then how do we get out?" Veyrina demanded, her voice rising despite the panic creeping into her chest. "You said there was a way. Tell us—what do we have to do to leave this place?"

Maelithra's eyes flickered with something darker, something almost regretful. "The path to freedom is not simple. You both must understand—freedom comes at a cost. One of you must let go of the other. Only then will the bond be severed, and only then will the echo realm release you. If you refuse to choose, then you will both remain here forever, trapped by the very thing you cherish the most."

Elyndra took a shaky step forward, her eyes wide with disbelief. "No. There has to be another way."

"There isn't." Maelithra's voice was firm, the finality of her words cutting through the tension like a blade. "I have been here too long to lie. I've seen countless souls who've tried to escape. They all paid the price for their defiance."

Elyndra turned to Veyrina, her eyes searching, as though looking for something to hold on to—some glimmer of hope that wasn't being shattered in front of them. "We can't let go of each other, Veyrina. I won't. You mean everything to me. This place… this realm, it's trying to tear us apart. I know it is. But I won't give in."

Veyrina's heart twisted painfully. She wanted to believe Elyndra, wanted to think that there was some way out, some secret to be uncovered that would allow them to escape without the heart-wrenching sacrifice that Maelithra was demanding. But deep down, she knew that the woman who stood before them—who had once shared a bond with Elyndra—was not lying.

"Then why are you still here?" Veyrina asked, her voice quieter now, filled with a mixture of fear and frustration. "Why haven't you escaped, Maelithra? Why are you still bound to this place if you knew the cost?"

Maelithra's eyes hardened, her lips pressing into a thin line. "Because I failed. I made my choice, and now I am bound here to pay the price. I thought I could hold on to my love—thought I could fight the forces of this realm. But I was wrong." Her voice cracked as she spoke the next words. "Now, I seek redemption. I cannot leave until one of you makes the ultimate sacrifice. You see, the bond you share is both a gift and a curse. The love that connects you, that fuels this realm… it is what you must give up to escape."

The silence that followed was deafening. Veyrina could hear her heart beating in her ears, each pulse a reminder of how impossible this decision was. Elyndra, too, seemed paralyzed by the weight of the choice that loomed over them. The thought of walking away from each other, of losing everything they had fought for—it was unbearable.

Elyndra's voice broke the silence, but it was a hollow, strained whisper. "I won't. I can't let you—"

"Think about it," Maelithra interrupted, her voice cold, sharp. "Think about the future you want. The life you crave. It is possible. But only if you're willing to sever the bond that ties you together. Only if one of you is willing to walk away."

Veyrina's gaze locked with Elyndra's, and for the first time, she saw the fear in Elyndra's eyes—a fear that mirrored her own. They had been through so much together, survived countless trials, and fought through impossible odds to be here, in this moment. The thought of abandoning everything, of losing each other forever, was too much to bear. Yet, they could not ignore the truth that Maelithra had laid bare.

"I don't want to lose you," Veyrina whispered, her voice cracking with emotion.

Elyndra's eyes softened, and for a moment, the harshness of the situation seemed to fade. They stood in that heavy silence, the weight of their shared love pressing against them like an invisible force. The fire in the sky flickered, the desert stretched endlessly before them, and the frozen sea shimmered under the heat of the burning sun. It was as if the very realm was alive, watching them, waiting for their decision.

Maelithra stepped back, folding her arms across her chest, her dark gaze never leaving them. "The trial has been set. The realm is waiting. The choice is yours."

The two women stood facing each other, the bond between them more palpable than ever. Veyrina's heart ached, knowing the devastating choice they were being asked to make. They were being tested, pushed to their limits, forced to confront the very thing that had brought them together—and could now tear them apart.

Elyndra took a deep breath, her chest rising and falling with the effort to steady herself. "We can't let this realm control us. We can't let it dictate our fate."

"Then we have to make the hardest choice," Veyrina said softly, her voice filled with both determination and sorrow. "But we will make it together. We won't give up on each other— not now. Not ever."

The words felt like a promise, a vow made under the weight of an impossible decision. But deep within Veyrina, a flicker of something began to burn—a light, faint but unyielding. She didn't know what would come next, or how they would escape the tangled web of fate they had found themselves in, but one thing was certain: they would face whatever came next together.

No matter the cost.

The air seemed to thicken around them as the gravity of their unspoken promise settled into place. Elyndra's fingers brushed against Veyrina's, the brief touch like a spark in the midst of the swirling storm of their emotions. The weight of their decision loomed larger than the unforgiving landscapes stretching out around them.

Veyrina glanced back at Maelithra, her heart hammering. "What do you mean when you say the realm is waiting? What happens if we refuse?"

Maelithra's lips curled into something that could have been a bitter smile. "Refusal has consequences, but not for me. Not for those who have already failed." Her eyes flickered toward the horizon where the sky seemed to shimmer unnaturally, as if bending time itself. "The realm does not care for your choices. It feeds off your indecision, your uncertainty. It is a place of endless loops, of souls trapped in cycles of their own making."

Veyrina shuddered. The thought of becoming another lost soul, another fragment of time wandering without purpose, made her stomach churn. She squeezed Elyndra's hand, the touch grounding her as much as it could.

Elyndra's eyes were fixed on Maelithra, her expression set.

"What's stopping us from finding a different way? There has to be another path."

Maelithra's gaze softened, but the sadness in her eyes was palpable. "There is no other way, Elyndra. Trust me, I've searched for it. The only way to sever the bond between you two is through sacrifice—one of you must choose to leave the other behind."

The words hit them both like a slap, and for a moment, they stood in silence, overwhelmed by the enormity of the choice that had been laid before them.

Elyndra looked down, her brow furrowing. "Why… why would I choose to leave her? How can I walk away from the one person who means everything to me?"

Veyrina's throat tightened, her heart echoing Elyndra's anguish. The thought of losing her, of severing the bond they had fought so hard to preserve, was unimaginable. Yet, the reality was undeniable. If they couldn't escape this realm, if they didn't make the choice, they would be trapped forever.

"Because," Maelithra interrupted, "you are both bound to this realm by a force far stronger than either of you can comprehend. The only way to break free is to let go. Only one can pass through the portal, only one can claim freedom. The other must stay behind."

Elyndra turned away, her chest heaving with the weight of her thoughts. The frozen seas beyond them glittered in the dim light, an eerily beautiful scene that only deepened the ache in her heart. Her thoughts were swirling—too many emotions, too many choices—but one thing was clear: Veyrina was everything to her.

"I can't do it," Elyndra whispered, her voice breaking. "I can't choose. I can't leave you behind."

Veyrina's fingers trembled in Elyndra's, the pulse between them more electric than ever before. Her heart was heavy, but her resolve began to harden like steel. "We don't have to choose. We don't have to listen to her, Elyndra."

But even as the words left her mouth, doubt crept in. Maelithra's warning still rang in her ears, louder than anything she could say. Refuse the choice, and they would both be lost. The uncertainty gnawed at her like a feral thing.

"I don't want to lose you," Veyrina whispered. "But I can't live trapped here forever. I can't bear to think of never seeing you again. I… I don't know what to do."

Elyndra's grip tightened around her hand, and for a moment, they stood there, the world around them turning into a blur of chaos and endless despair. Every part of Veyrina wanted to scream, to fight against the impossible choice before them. But the weight of Maelithra's words held her fast, like a spell woven around them.

"Maybe…" Elyndra's voice faltered, then strengthened. "Maybe it's not about choosing between us. Maybe it's about trusting that whatever happens, we'll find our way back to each other."

Veyrina's breath caught in her throat. Could it be that simple? Could it be that the strength of their bond—of the love they had fought for—could transcend even this?

But Maelithra's voice cut through their thoughts once again, sharp and cutting. "You are naïve if you believe that. The Unseen Realm will take what it is owed, one way or another. You cannot fight fate."

For a heartbeat, the landscape seemed to shift around them. The sky darkened, as if the realm itself were reacting to the tension in the air. The winds howled louder, the ice beneath their feet cracking and shifting, as if the very foundations of the world were crumbling.

Elyndra stepped forward, her jaw set in quiet defiance. "We'll find a way, Veyrina. We've faced worse than this. We're stronger than they think."

Veyrina followed her lead, her heart swelling with a renewed sense of determination. "Yes. We are stronger. And I won't let them tear us apart."

The world around them seemed to pulse, as if reacting to their resolve. The frozen sea shimmered, the burning sky overhead flickering with unnatural intensity. But no matter how hard the realm tried to break them, they refused to bend.

And then, Maelithra's expression shifted, her eyes narrowing in an unreadable gaze. "Then prove it," she said. "Prove to me that your bond is strong enough to survive the trial."

Before Veyrina or Elyndra could respond, the ground beneath them began to tremble. The swirling desert sands parted like a wound, revealing a massive chasm—a black void that seemed to stretch endlessly down into the depths of the realm. Dark tendrils of smoke spiraled from its edges, and from within the abyss, an eerie, familiar voice whispered.

"One must descend into the darkness to find the truth. Only then will the bond be tested."

The voice echoed through the chasm, and Veyrina felt her skin prickle with unease. "What is this place?"

Maelithra stepped back, a haunted expression crossing her face. "It is the trial. You must face the abyss. The darkness that lies within you both. Only by confronting your deepest fears will you prove that your bond can survive."

Elyndra took a slow, steady breath, her voice a whisper, filled with a mix of fear and determination. "Then let's face it together."

Veyrina nodded, squeezing her hand. "Together, always."

And with that, they took their first step toward the abyss, not knowing what horrors awaited them in the darkness below. But one thing was clear: the love they shared would be tested. And they would not go down without a fight.

Thirteen

Fractured Memories

The air grew colder as Veyrina and Elyndra ventured deeper into the Unseen Realm. The world around them seemed to fold in on itself, the landscapes shifting in ways that defied logic. Frozen lakes stretched endlessly in one direction, while burning mountains reached for a sky that bled shades of violet and crimson. It was a world born of fractured time, where nothing made sense, and everything felt like a dream they could not escape.

Elyndra walked beside Veyrina, her fingers brushing against the cool stone of the path beneath them, but there was an unsettled energy in the air. Something about the realm gnawed at her, the weight of the unknown pressing heavily against her chest. Her heart, which had once felt so sure, now fluttered with uncertainty. She couldn't shake the feeling that they were being watched, that every step they took was being measured, weighed. The echoes of their past had already begun to follow them, subtle whispers of memories not their own.

"Do you feel it?" Elyndra asked, her voice barely above a whisper.

Veyrina nodded, her eyes narrowing as she scanned their surroundings. "Yes. It's like the air is thick with something… wrong."

The ground shifted beneath them, and a ripple of energy coursed through the air, distorting the horizon like a broken mirror. It was as though the very fabric of this world was unraveling before their eyes. The tension between them grew palpable as the landscape twisted, blending the past and the present in ways that felt impossible.

Suddenly, the world around them froze. The air went still, heavy with a sense of dread. Veyrina and Elyndra stopped in their tracks, their hearts racing in unison. The sound of distant voices echoed through the silence, faint but clear, like whispers on the wind.

"I… I remember this," Elyndra murmured, her voice trembling. "This place, these faces… they're familiar."

Veyrina turned to her, her brow furrowing. "What do you mean? What do you remember?"

Elyndra closed her eyes, a faint shimmer of recollection flashing across her expression. "I see us, but not like this… not like now. I see us in different lives, in different times. But… why does it feel like it's all slipping through my fingers?"

Before Veyrina could respond, a sharp pain pierced her head, a sudden flash of images flooding her mind. Memories, not her own, crashing over her like a tide. The face of a man— handsome, yet cold—gazed down at her with an expression of indifference. She saw herself, dressed in fine clothes, standing beside him in a grand hall. His eyes were empty, devoid of emotion, and yet she could feel the weight of the connection between them.

What is this?

The question echoed in her mind, but there was no answer. The memories continued to spiral, disjointed and fragmented. She saw a scene of betrayal, a sharp knife pressed against someone's throat—was it her? The man, the one whose face haunted her, spoke words that she couldn't quite understand, his voice drowned in the rush of the images. But the feeling of pain, of loss, was clear.

Then, just as suddenly as it had begun, the vision shattered. Veyrina staggered, her breath ragged as the cold sweat dripped down her face. She blinked rapidly, trying to steady herself, but the lingering effects of the memories clung to her like shadows.

"Elyndra…" she whispered, her voice barely audible. "What's happening? What are these memories?"

Elyndra's face was pale, her eyes wide with a mix of confusion and fear. "I… I don't know. But I saw it too. I saw the same man. And I—I felt it. I felt what we were… what we could have been. But it wasn't us, not really."

Veyrina's heart skipped a beat. "It wasn't us?" she echoed, her mind racing. "Then what is it? What are we, Elyndra?"

The silence between them was thick with unspoken words, the weight of their shared confusion hanging in the air like an oppressive storm cloud. The memories they had just glimpsed were not their own, yet they felt like a part of them, tangled in the threads of their existence. Were they trapped in some twisted version of fate, bound to experience lives they had never lived?

Before Elyndra could respond, another vision overtook them, this one more vivid, more real. Veyrina's body tensed as the images swept over her, consuming her consciousness. She saw herself standing alone on a cliffside, her hands clenched into fists as she stared down at the churning sea below. There was a storm brewing, the winds howling around her as the waves crashed against the rocks.

And then, as if summoned by the intensity of her emotions, the figure of the man appeared. He stood at a distance, watching her with a cold, impassive expression. His presence was suffocating, his gaze like a weight on her chest.

"You can never escape it," the man's voice rang out, deep and gravelly, a voice that carried the weight of countless lifetimes. "The truth is always there, buried beneath the surface. You will never outrun your fate."

Veyrina's heart thudded in her chest as she watched him, her entire body trembling with fear. "No," she whispered. "I won't be bound to this. I won't."

But the man's eyes never wavered. "You are already bound. And this—" He gestured to the swirling storm around them. "This is just the beginning."

With a final, cruel smile, he vanished into the storm, leaving her alone once more, the weight of his words hanging in the air like a curse.

The vision shattered, leaving Veyrina gasping for air. She collapsed to her knees, her hands trembling as she struggled to make sense of what she had just experienced. It wasn't just a memory—it was a warning. A truth she was not yet ready to face.

"Elyndra," she choked out, her voice raw with emotion. "I don't understand. What is this place? What does it want from us?"

Elyndra crouched beside her, her own expression haunted.

"I don't know, but I feel it too. These memories, these visions… they don't feel like ours. They're fragments, echoes of lives we never lived but could have."

Veyrina's mind raced. "But why show us these things? Why now?"

"I think it's trying to tear us apart," Elyndra whispered. "To make us doubt what we've fought for. It's planting seeds of doubt in our hearts, trying to convince us that our love is a lie. That we were never meant to be."

The weight of her words settled between them, heavy and suffocating. Veyrina's heart ached at the thought. Could it be true? Could their love have always been a lie, a cruel trick played by the Unseen Realm to keep them trapped here?

Before she could voice the question that lingered in her mind, a cold wind whipped through the air, and the landscape around them shifted once more. The ground trembled beneath their feet, and a deep rumbling echoed from somewhere within the realm. A shadow, dark and formless, appeared before them, its presence sending a chill of fear down their spines.

The figure was an indistinct shape at first, but as it drew closer, it took on a more tangible form—an entity born of the realm's twisted magic. It was a being of pure darkness, its eyes glowing with an otherworldly fire as it stepped into their path. The air around it crackled with power, and the ground beneath its feet began to crack and splinter.

"You cannot escape," the entity's voice echoed, hollow and resonant, like a thousand voices speaking as one. "You are bound to this place, just as you are bound to the memories it holds. Face the truth—your love was never meant to be. You are nothing more than fragments of a broken past."

Veyrina's breath caught in her throat. "No… you're lying."

The entity tilted its head, its gaze never leaving them. "Am I? Or are you just too afraid to see the truth? You were never meant to be together. You were never meant to break the chains that bind you."

With a flick of its hand, the ground around them trembled, and more visions flashed before their eyes—more memories of lives they had never lived, of loves they had never known, of betrayals and sacrifices that seemed to intertwine with their own.

Veyrina's knees buckled beneath her, the weight of the memories crashing over her once more. "Elyndra," she gasped. "Is it true? Were we never meant to be?"

Elyndra's hand gripped hers tightly. "No. We are meant to be. We have to believe that. Together, we can face whatever this realm throws at us."

But even as she said the words, Veyrina felt the tendrils of doubt creeping into her heart. Would their love truly survive the fractures of their past? Or was it already shattered beyond repair?

The entity loomed before them, its presence suffocating the very air. The ground beneath their feet seemed to pulse, as if the world itself was aware of the tension between them. Elyndra tightened her grip on Veyrina's hand, her fingers trembling, though she refused to let go. Her breath came in ragged gasps, but there was something else burning in her— something fierce, something that refused to break. Despite the overwhelming doubt, despite the weight of the fractured memories that plagued them both, Elyndra had one certainty left: she would fight for them. She would fight for Veyrina.

"Do not listen to it," Elyndra said, her voice barely more than a whisper, but it was firm, unwavering. "We are not bound by these broken fragments. We are not the echoes it wants us to be. We are something more."

Veyrina turned to her, her heart aching at the sight of the vulnerability in Elyndra's eyes. She wanted to believe those words with every fiber of her being, but the remnants of the visions, the memories that refused to stay buried, twisted around her like vines of doubt. She could still feel the weight of the betrayal, the coldness of the man in the vision, the storm that had swallowed her soul whole.

"You don't understand," Veyrina breathed, her voice shaking as she struggled to meet Elyndra's gaze. "I saw it. I saw us, but not like this. We were… different. We were broken in ways I can't explain. I'm scared, Elyndra. What if we were never meant to be together? What if we were just… another failed attempt, another lost fragment in this endless cycle?"

Her words hung between them, a confession that felt like a poison on her tongue. She could see the pain flicker in Elyndra's eyes, but there was no judgment. Only understanding. Still, Veyrina couldn't shake the feeling that the memories—no matter how fragmented—were leading them down a path they could not return from.

"Don't you see?" Elyndra's voice cracked with raw emotion, her hand reaching out to touch Veyrina's face. "These memories… they aren't ours. They're not ours to carry. They're the lies the realm wants us to believe. This place is trying to break us apart, but we're stronger than it knows. We can fight it together. We will fight it together."

The shadows that surrounded them seemed to stir, as if responding to their words. The entity's laughter echoed through the space, hollow and unnerving.

"You think you can defy fate?" The voice was like an avalanche, its power crashing down around them. "You have seen the truth now. You are nothing more than echoes, mere shadows of lives that were never truly yours. Every love you feel, every connection you make—it's all a lie. And you will never escape it."

The ground beneath their feet trembled, and suddenly, the earth split open in front of them, revealing a chasm that stretched into the depths of the void. The sound of cracking stone filled the air as fissures ran across the land. The realm itself seemed to be pulling them into the abyss.

Elyndra stepped forward, pulling Veyrina with her. "No. We will not fall. Not now."

The entity, seemingly delighted by their defiance, reached out with its dark hand, the air crackling as it attempted to tear them apart with sheer force. "Foolish girls. You cannot escape what you are. You cannot escape me."

With a sudden surge of energy, Veyrina and Elyndra were thrown backward, their bodies slamming into the jagged rocks that lined the edges of the chasm. Pain lanced through them, but the force of it was momentarily grounding, clearing the fog of doubt from their minds. They had been brought to this point for a reason, and they would not let the shadows of their past define them any longer.

Veyrina gasped for breath as she struggled to rise, her hands pressing against the cold stone. She turned to Elyndra, her eyes wide with a mixture of fear and determination. "What if we fail?" she whispered, her voice trembling. "What if we're not strong enough?"

Elyndra reached out, her fingers brushing against Veyrina's cheek, grounding her. The warmth of Elyndra's touch cut through the cold, and Veyrina felt something shift within her—a spark of clarity that burned away the shadows. It was a feeling she had never been able to explain, a connection that transcended time and space.

"You are stronger than you think," Elyndra said, her voice fierce now. "We are stronger than this realm, stronger than any lie it tries to weave. Our love is real, Veyrina. And that is the one thing the Unseen Realm cannot touch. We will face this together. Always."

Tears filled Veyrina's eyes, but they weren't born of fear. They were tears of recognition—of understanding. The truth, the one that had been hidden beneath the fractured memories, was clear now. Their love was not an illusion. It had never been an illusion. It was the only thing that was truly theirs, the only thing that mattered.

With renewed strength, they rose to their feet. The entity loomed before them, its dark presence still pressing in, but they were no longer afraid. Together, they stepped toward it, hand in hand, ready to confront whatever darkness it had in store.

The entity's form flickered, a flicker of doubt creeping into its expression. "You defy fate? You challenge the very essence of what you are?"

"Yes," Elyndra said, her voice unwavering. "We do."

"And you will regret it," the entity hissed, its voice like a storm on the horizon. "You cannot escape what is already written."

Veyrina and Elyndra stood their ground. The air around them began to shift, the crackling tension in the realm fading as the power they had unlocked together began to swell. The fractures in their hearts, in their minds, began to mend, slowly but surely. The darkness that had surrounded them began to recede, unable to withstand the force of their love.

"You're wrong," Veyrina said, her voice strong. "We are not echoes. We are not bound by what came before us. We are what we choose to be."

The entity faltered, its form flickering once more. Its eyes, glowing with an unsettling fire, seemed to flicker with uncertainty. For the first time, it hesitated.

"We… we choose each other," Elyndra added, her voice soft but filled with conviction. "And nothing can take that from us."

A final, thunderous crack split the air as the realm around them trembled. The chasm began to close, the dark entity shrieking in frustration, its form collapsing inward, the shadows scattering like smoke in the wind.

As the darkness retreated, Veyrina and Elyndra stood, breathing heavily but victorious. The chasm closed, the ground beneath them solidifying once more. The Unseen Realm, which had once seemed so hostile, now felt… different. It was as if their combined will had altered its very fabric.

In the silence that followed, they stood together, their hands still intertwined. The air was no longer heavy with doubt, but with a quiet, resolute peace. They had faced their fractured memories, their fears, and come out stronger.

Veyrina turned to Elyndra, her eyes filled with a quiet gratitude. "You were right. I was scared. But you showed me the way. You gave me the strength to believe in us."

Elyndra smiled, her eyes shining with affection. "We're not just surviving, Veyrina. We're thriving. Together."

The world around them seemed to breathe a little easier, the chaos of the Unseen Realm momentarily subdued. They had passed the trial, not just of this place, but of their love. And now, as they faced the uncertain future that awaited them, they knew one thing above all else: no matter what lay ahead, they would face it together.

And that, Veyrina realized, was the truest freedom of all.

Fourteen

The Heart's Labyrinth

The air in the Unseen Realm had thickened, heavy with an oppressive silence that seemed to echo with every breath Veyrina took. They had traveled through landscapes both haunting and alien, but nothing had prepared them for what lay ahead. In front of them, nestled among twisted, dark trees with gnarled branches reaching toward a starless sky, was a vast, shifting labyrinth.

Its walls were tall and made of what looked like living shadows, shifting and warping in the dark, whispering with faint voices that carried a sense of foreboding. Veyrina's heart began to pound as the weight of the labyrinth pressed upon them.

"This… this is it, isn't it?" Elyndra whispered, her voice barely more than a breath.

Veyrina didn't need to ask what Elyndra meant. They both understood that the labyrinth was not just a physical maze—it was a representation of everything they had struggled with, a trial for their hearts and souls.

"We have no choice but to go through," Veyrina said, her tone steady even as the storm within her raged.

Elyndra nodded, her dark eyes scanning the labyrinth's entrance as if searching for an escape she knew would not come. Her steps were slow, as though she had already seen the price that might come with navigating the maze.

They stepped into the labyrinth, and the walls closed in behind them, the sounds of the world outside vanishing into an eerie, suffocating silence. The air felt colder now, biting at their skin, and the ground beneath their feet seemed to shift with every step, making it impossible to get a clear sense of direction.

The walls were alive, pulsating with a strange energy, and the paths twisted in strange angles, creating an unending sense of disorientation. It wasn't just the physical space that was disorienting—it was the weight of the echoes that lingered, faint at first but growing louder with every step. The whispers of memories, fractured and distorted, clawed at their minds.

Suddenly, the first shadow appeared—Elyndra's own reflection, but it was wrong. The figure that stood before them was tall and regal, a darkened version of Elyndra, but her eyes were cold, calculating, cruel.

"It's time you faced the truth, Elyndra," the shadow hissed, its voice a mocking echo of her own. "You were always the one who abandoned me. Your love was never enough. Look at the path you've walked—the pain you've caused. It was all your fault."

Elyndra froze, her heart skipping in her chest. She turned away, but the shadow was right there, its form shifting like liquid darkness, twisting in ways that made it seem to grow with every second.

"Tell me it's not true, Elyndra," the shadow purred, its voice like a knife. "Tell me you didn't betray us both, again and again."

Veyrina could feel Elyndra's turmoil, the way the words cut deep into her soul. She stepped forward, reaching for Elyndra's hand, but when she touched her, the shadow of Elyndra turned its gaze toward her.

"And what about you, Veyrina?" the shadow hissed, its face melting into something even more sinister. "Do you think she's worth all this? Do you think she deserves your love? How many times have you stood by her, only to be betrayed by her in return? How long will you be her fool?"

The words hit Veyrina like a physical blow. She staggered back, but the labyrinth shifted again, disorienting her, making her dizzy. She looked back at Elyndra, but the shadowy figure of her love seemed to be retreating into the darkness, leaving her alone.

"Veyrina!" Elyndra called out, her voice trembling.

Veyrina snapped back to attention. The labyrinth's walls pressed in even tighter, like the very air was suffocating them. They had to keep moving.

Elyndra reached for her, her hand shaking, but the labyrinth's energy seemed to push them apart. It was as though the very air was charged with the power to rip them from each other's grasp.

The shadows of the past continued to press in, each step forward causing new echoes of their previous lives to rear their twisted heads—old lovers, betrayals, moments of love lost, forgotten promises. With each step, it felt like a part of them was unraveling, their past selves bleeding through the cracks of the labyrinth, each shadow pulling them farther from each other.

"We need to keep going," Elyndra said, her voice barely audible.

Veyrina nodded, gripping her hand tighter. They moved forward together, but the further they walked, the more the labyrinth seemed to tighten around them, the shadows becoming more solid, more oppressive.

They encountered another figure—a ghostly version of Veyrina's own past, an image of someone she had loved in a life she didn't fully remember.

The figure was a woman—tall and regal with burning eyes that seemed to know every dark secret Veyrina had buried within herself. "So, this is how it ends?" the woman mocked. "Are you really willing to keep walking down this same path, Veyrina? Again and again, you'll return to her, and it will all be the same. A cycle of love, loss, betrayal. You're too weak to escape it. You'll always come back."

The woman's voice was like the wind, sharp and biting. The words tore at the edges of Veyrina's resolve, but she gritted her teeth and pushed forward, keeping her focus on Elyndra, the one constant she had left.

"We are not like them," Elyndra said, her voice filled with quiet strength. "We have the power to change this. We've always had the power."

Veyrina met her gaze, her heart beating louder than the labyrinth's shifting walls. Elyndra's words seemed to reverberate through the very core of her being. She reached for Elyndra's hand again, and this time, the shadows didn't pull them apart. Their hands clasped, fingers intertwining, and for a moment, the labyrinth seemed to hold its breath.

"Together," Veyrina whispered. "We can face this. Together."

The labyrinth shuddered, the walls seeming to pause in their relentless shifting. For the first time, the echoes faded into silence, and the shadows seemed to fade, dissolving into nothingness.

But even as the darkness began to recede, another figure appeared before them. A shadow darker than the rest, an ominous presence that lingered, twisted and malevolent. This was no mere memory—it was the manifestation of their fear, of everything they had ever avoided.

"I will not let you escape," the figure rasped, its voice deeper, more menacing. It towered over them, a monster made from their very doubts, fears, and regrets. "Not without paying the price for everything you have done, for every love you've lost."

The final trial had come. The true test was not just escaping the labyrinth—it was surviving the fear of the truth they had hidden from each other, from themselves.

Veyrina stepped forward, her breath catching in her throat. "We've already lost enough. We don't have to lose each other."

And with that, she plunged into the heart of the labyrinth, her hand still holding tightly to Elyndra's. The world shifted, the shadows dissipating, and they entered the final space of the labyrinth—a clearing at the center, where the echoes of their love stood before them, trembling and fractured, ready to face the ultimate trial.

The question now was simple: Could they forgive themselves? Could they forgive each other? Or would they be lost forever in the maze of their own creation?

As Veyrina and Elyndra stepped deeper into the heart of the labyrinth, the air grew colder still, biting at their skin with an unnatural chill that seeped into their bones. The world around them seemed to stretch out, warping and flickering like a broken mirror, each reflection fractured and imperfect. The walls, once shadowy and oppressive, now seemed to dissolve into the ether itself, leaving them standing in a vast, empty expanse.

In this space, the silence was deafening. Every breath they took reverberated with the weight of their unspoken fears and doubts. Veyrina could feel Elyndra's grip on her hand tighten, as though she, too, was bracing for the inevitable. The silence stretched on, broken only by the faintest whispers of voices from the past.

Suddenly, before them, a figure appeared—a ghostly silhouette emerging from the mist that surrounded the clearing. This figure was unlike the others they had encountered in the labyrinth. There was no shadowy distortion, no taunting voice. It was Elyndra, but not the Elyndra standing next to her.

It was a version of her from the past, a younger self with eyes filled with an emptiness Veyrina had never seen before.

The figure stood there, unmoving, as if waiting for them to approach. It wasn't until Elyndra took a hesitant step forward that the air seemed to shift, becoming heavier and more oppressive.

"This is where it all started, isn't it?" the figure said, its voice calm and eerily familiar, yet distant. "You don't belong here, Elyndra. Not in this world, not with her."

Elyndra's face tightened as the words pierced through the air like arrows, each one finding its mark. The younger version of herself continued, its voice tinged with sorrow and regret.

"You think you can change your fate, that love will be enough to undo everything you've done. But it's not. You've always been destined to leave—just as you did before."

The shadows in the air thickened as the figure spoke, and Elyndra took a step back, her breath hitching in her throat. Veyrina could feel her lover's pulse quicken, the tension radiating off her body as she struggled to stay composed. It was as if the labyrinth itself had conjured her worst fears— Elyndra's deepest insecurities manifesting in the form of a past she could not escape.

Veyrina stepped forward, her resolve hardening. "You're wrong," she said, her voice steady, but carrying an undeniable undercurrent of emotion. "We're not the same people we were then. We've changed, and so has our love."

But the figure didn't move, its eyes locked on Elyndra as it spoke again, the words more cruel now.

"Love cannot save you," the figure sneered, the bitterness in its tone seeping into the very ground beneath them. "Not when it's built on lies, not when it's built on regrets."

The words struck at Elyndra's heart, and she staggered back, her eyes closing as she sought to escape the pain that gnawed at her. The labyrinth seemed to pulse with a malevolent energy, the walls around them closing in once again, suffocating them with the weight of the past.

For a moment, Elyndra was lost in the past, a place where pain and betrayal had shaped her every step. Her breath caught, and she whispered, "I never meant to hurt you, Veyrina."

The admission tore through Veyrina's chest, a jagged shard of truth that made her ache with an intensity she hadn't expected. She reached out, her fingers brushing Elyndra's arm, feeling the trembling warmth of her skin.

"Elyndra," Veyrina whispered, her voice breaking through the chaos. "We've both made mistakes. But we've always been here. We've always chosen each other, even when the world tried to tear us apart."

The figure flickered, its edges warping as it seemed to pull away, vanishing into the shadows. But the pain lingered, the wounds from their past still fresh in the air between them.

Elyndra opened her eyes, her gaze meeting Veyrina's with a mixture of sorrow and hope. "I'm afraid," Elyndra confessed, her voice quiet, yet strong. "Afraid that our love isn't enough. That we're just echoes in this labyrinth, never meant to escape."

Veyrina stepped forward, her heart aching with the weight of the words. "I used to be afraid too," she admitted. "Afraid of losing you, afraid of the things we couldn't change. But I've learned that love isn't about perfection. It's about choosing each other, again and again, no matter the cost."

The words hung in the air, vibrating with the power of truth, and the labyrinth seemed to pause, the tension in the air dissipating like fog under the first rays of sunlight. Veyrina's hand tightened around Elyndra's, and together, they moved forward, deeper into the heart of the labyrinth.

But the final test awaited them. As they ventured deeper, the walls of the labyrinth began to shift once again, and they were no longer alone. The ground beneath their feet began to tremble, the air thick with a sense of impending danger. The shadows returned, growing larger and more menacing, each one echoing with the voices of past regrets and unresolved pain.

Veyrina's pulse quickened as she glanced around, feeling the weight of the labyrinth's pressure building. The walls twisted and distorted, opening into a vast, infinite space that seemed to stretch beyond time itself. In the center of the room stood a dark figure, its form cloaked in shadows, radiating an aura of malevolence.

This was no simple specter. This was the manifestation of their greatest fears, their deepest regrets, and the true heart of the labyrinth.

"You cannot escape," the figure rasped, its voice a deep, unsettling growl that reverberated through the very core of their being. "You've walked this path before, and you will walk it again, trapped in the cycle of your own creation."

Veyrina stepped forward, her heart pounding in her chest. "We've already faced our past. We've already chosen to forgive ourselves."

The figure's eyes glowed with an unnatural light, and for a moment, it seemed to shimmer like smoke in the wind. "Forgiveness is not enough," the figure hissed. "Not when the past is so deeply ingrained in your souls. You cannot outrun what you've done."

But Veyrina and Elyndra stood firm, their hands still clasped tightly together. They had been through the fire of their own guilt and sorrow. They had lived through the echoes of their past lives, the brokenness that had shaped them, but they had never wavered from their choice.

And in that moment, the labyrinth seemed to hold its breath.

"You will never be free," the figure continued, its voice like ice, "Until you give up the one thing you hold most dear."

Veyrina's heart lurched. "What?" she demanded. "What are you talking about?"

The figure's form twisted, revealing a reflection of themselves, a fractured image of what they could have been—broken, separated, lost to the shadows forever. "You must choose, Veyrina. Choose to leave the labyrinth or choose to remain forever with her."

The air seemed to pulse with an unbearable weight. Elyndra's breath hitched as the reality of the choice laid itself bare before them. The labyrinth had always been more than just a physical maze—it was a test of their deepest, most vulnerable selves.

But Veyrina knew, with a certainty that burned in her chest, that they had already made the only choice that mattered.

"We choose each other," Veyrina said, her voice steady and unwavering.

The labyrinth trembled around them, its walls collapsing into nothingness. And together, they stepped forward, breaking free from the past that had held them captive, and into the light of their shared future.

Fifteen

The Price of Sacrifice

The labyrinth had crumbled behind them, its twisting corridors and haunting shadows nothing more than a fading memory now. As Veyrina and Elyndra emerged into the open expanse beyond the maze, the weight of the past seemed to lift from their shoulders. But the feeling of relief was short-lived. The air around them hummed with an unnatural vibration, as though the very fabric of the Unseen Realm was beginning to tear apart at the seams.

The sky above them was darkening, clouds swirling in ominous patterns, crackling with strange, violet lightning. The ground beneath their feet shuddered, sending ripples through the once-still landscape, now fractured and unstable. The labyrinth's collapse had triggered something—something far more dangerous than the trials they had already endured.

As they moved forward, the world around them shifted, changing in subtle ways that made Veyrina's heart race. The landscapes that had seemed so chaotic and untamed moments before now appeared even more distorted. Everything was coming undone. The echoes, once distant, now surged with raw, unbridled power, pushing and pulling at their minds like a magnetic force.

Elyndra's hand tightened around Veyrina's, her breath shallow as she tried to steady herself. "We have to keep going," she murmured, her voice strained but resolute. "The echo is collapsing. If we don't get out of here soon—"

"I know," Veyrina interrupted, squeezing her hand in reassurance. But even as she spoke, she could feel the tremors beneath their feet growing stronger, threatening to swallow them whole.

The air grew colder, the temperature dropping so suddenly that Veyrina felt as if the very blood in her veins had turned to ice. And then, from the darkness before them, a figure appeared. Tall and shrouded in shadow, the figure radiated an ancient, otherworldly presence. His form was ethereal, almost translucent, as though he were both part of the world and entirely separate from it.

The figure's eyes gleamed with an unsettling light, shifting colors like liquid fire. He stood motionless for a long moment, studying them with an intensity that made Veyrina's skin crawl.

"You have come far," the figure's voice rang out, deep and resonant, echoing through the decaying air. "But this is where your journey ends, unless you are willing to make a choice."

Veyrina's heart skipped a beat, and Elyndra stiffened beside her. "Who are you?" Veyrina demanded, her voice sharp with distrust.

The figure's lips curled into a faint, knowing smile. "I am Ithranos Melaes, an ancient entity, a keeper of the realms beyond time. You stand at the threshold of your future, but before you can pass through, you must decide what you are willing to sacrifice."

Elyndra took a step forward, her face filled with confusion and apprehension. "What are you talking about? We've made it this far—we're ready to leave. What more is there to face?"

Ithranos Melaes's smile deepened, his eyes glowing brighter. "The Unseen Realm was never meant to be a place of salvation," he explained. "It exists as a prison for those like you—trapped by the echoes of past lives, bound to repeat the cycles of love and loss. You have managed to break free from the labyrinth, but the echo still lingers. The realm itself is crumbling, and you must choose: break the cycle completely, or remain here, forever."

Veyrina's pulse quickened. "What do you mean, break the cycle?"

Ithranos raised a hand, and with it, the world around them shifted again. The sky darkened further, and the very ground beneath their feet seemed to tremble with the weight of unseen forces. "The echo that binds you," Ithranos continued, his voice growing heavier with each word, "it can be severed. But it will come at a great cost."

Veyrina's breath caught in her throat. "What cost?"

Ithranos's eyes glowed brighter, burning with an intensity that made the world around them feel small and insignificant. "One of you must remain here, lost in the echo for eternity. The other may return to the real world, free of the chains that bind you. You may never see each other again, nor feel the pull of the other's soul."

The words hung in the air like a thunderclap, reverberating with an intensity that stole the breath from Veyrina's lungs.

Elyndra's face blanched, her hand trembling in Veyrina's. The weight of the decision—of the sacrifice—hung between them like a chasm that could never be crossed.

"Why?" Elyndra asked, her voice barely above a whisper. "Why must it be this way?"

Ithranos's expression softened, though the pity in his gaze did little to ease the fear gnawing at their hearts. "Because the cycle of the echo has consumed too much of your essence. You cannot escape it without paying a price. If you choose freedom, one of you must remain here, bound by the echoes forever. If you both choose to stay, you will both be lost to the void, forgotten by time."

Veyrina felt her mind spin, her thoughts racing, struggling to find any solution, any way to escape this impossible choice. Every fiber of her being screamed to reject the idea, to demand a way out. But the truth was undeniable: the realm was unraveling, and the only way forward was through this impossible decision.

Elyndra's eyes met hers, filled with desperation. "Veyrina, I can't… I can't ask you to stay behind. Not after everything we've been through. You deserve to live your life, to be free of all this. If anyone should stay, it should be me."

"No," Veyrina breathed, shaking her head vehemently. "I won't leave you. We've already been through so much—this can't be how it ends. I won't make that choice. We don't have to be apart."

Ithranos watched them silently, his eyes piercing into their souls, reading their thoughts like an open book. "It is the only way. There is no other path forward."

The silence stretched on, the weight of the decision suffocating them both. Veyrina's mind spun with memories—of the moments they had shared, the love they had fought for, the future they had dreamed of. How could she choose between that future and the woman she loved?

"I will stay," Elyndra said, her voice breaking the silence like a shattered glass. "I'll stay so you can be free."

Veyrina's heart clenched, her vision blurring with unshed tears. "No… No, Elyndra. I won't lose you. I won't let you sacrifice yourself."

The air around them shimmered with a sudden intensity, as if the very fabric of reality were holding its breath. The walls of the Unseen Realm seemed to close in on them, a reminder that time was running out.

Ithranos's voice cut through the silence. "Choose now, or the realm will collapse entirely. You have but moments left."

The pressure mounted, suffocating, unrelenting. Veyrina closed her eyes, trying to force her racing thoughts into something coherent. The decision felt impossible, and yet, she knew—deep in her soul—that no matter what choice they made, it would be a choice that defined everything that came after.

"We can't escape the echo, can we?" Veyrina whispered, her voice trembling. "We can never truly escape it."

Ithranos did not answer, but the meaning in his silence was clear. The price of freedom was steep. The price of love was something no one should ever have to pay.

And in that moment, Veyrina knew there was only one thing left to do.

"We'll stay together," she said, her voice firm with a resolve that surprised even herself. "Whatever the cost. Whatever the sacrifice."

Elyndra's eyes softened, a tear slipping down her cheek. "But,

Veyrina, we can't—"

"I won't let you face this alone," Veyrina whispered, her grip tightening on Elyndra's hand. "We've always been together. We'll find a way, even if it means paying the ultimate price."

The world around them trembled, the reality of their choice crashing down upon them. The Unseen Realm seemed to pulse with energy, as if the very core of the realm recognized the strength of their decision. The echo that had once held them captive wavered, the thread of time stretching and snapping under the weight of their love.

And in that moment, as they stood together, facing the unknown, they realized that sometimes the greatest sacrifice wasn't in choosing what they could live without, but in choosing what they couldn't live without.

The world around them shattered. The echo ceased to exist.

And the price of their sacrifice was yet to be revealed.

As the echo of their decision reverberated through the fabric of the Unseen Realm, the landscape around them quivered and buckled, as though the realm itself was recoiling from the weight of their choice. The shadows of twisted, forgotten dreams, of lost loves and broken promises, began to flicker at the edges of Veyrina and Elyndra's vision, but they stood resolute. Their hands remained locked together, a physical manifestation of their unyielding commitment to one another.

The entity Ithranos Melaes did not move, but his presence seemed to thicken, as though he were both watching and waiting, his gaze unblinking and inscrutable.

"You have chosen," Ithranos's voice resonated through the crumbling void, deep and sonorous. "The price has been set. The fabric of the Unseen Realm will tear, and you shall be forever bound to the echo, though in a way you have not yet understood."

Veyrina's breath hitched. She could feel the strain of the decision, the burden of what it meant. But there was no turning back now. She glanced at Elyndra, who met her gaze with a look of equal determination. They had made their choice. Now, they would face the consequences together.

"We will endure," Elyndra whispered, her voice steady despite the chaos swirling around them.

The realm began to dissolve in waves, the sky shattering like glass as the very ground beneath their feet fractured. In the distance, the ruins of what had once been solid walls and corridors now crumbled into nothingness, as though the echoes of time were being swallowed by an insatiable void. The air shimmered and twisted as the last vestiges of reality unraveled around them, the entire Unseen Realm collapsing under the weight of their decision.

As the ground beneath their feet began to give way, Veyrina could feel the pull of something deeper, something primal, wrapping around her heart. It was the echo, relentless in its hunger. She could feel the dissonance between their souls and the world they had entered—a dissonance that had only grown stronger as they made their decision.

"This is not the end," Ithranos's voice rang out again, now more distant, as though it were coming from somewhere deep within the collapse. "It is merely the beginning of your trial. The true price of sacrifice is not always seen in the moment of choice, but in the time that follows."

"What do you mean?" Elyndra called, her voice strained as she fought against the disorienting tug of the unraveling world.

"The echo will not let you go so easily," Ithranos replied.

"It will test you. Your love, your resolve. You will face trials greater than the labyrinth, greater than anything you have yet endured. But only through these trials will you truly break free."

The world shifted again. The ground beneath their feet was gone, replaced by a dizzying expanse of swirling light and shadow. For a brief, breathless moment, Veyrina felt as though she were floating between worlds, suspended in time itself. The air was thick, as if it held every memory they had ever shared, every whispered promise and fleeting kiss.

And then, in the blink of an eye, the world solidified again, but this time, it was different. They stood in a vast, open space—an endless plain that stretched beyond the horizon. The sky above them was an unsettling shade of deep violet, tinged with the faint glow of distant stars. The ground was cracked and barren, with no sign of life anywhere. It felt empty, almost like a dream suspended in time.

Veyrina and Elyndra turned slowly, taking in their new surroundings. It was as though they had been dropped into another version of the Unseen Realm—one even more desolate and unwelcoming.

"Where are we?" Veyrina whispered, her voice filled with awe and fear.

"This is the next trial," Ithranos's voice echoed, coming from all around them now. "The cost has been paid. You are here, together, but you are not yet free."

A sudden gust of wind swept across the barren plain, stirring the dust and sand at their feet. In the distance, the shape of a figure emerged from the swirling haze. It was an indistinct silhouette at first, but as it drew closer, Veyrina's heart skipped a beat. The figure was familiar—too familiar. It was an image of herself, or a twisted version of herself, shadowed and shifting in the dim light.

"No…" Veyrina gasped, stepping back in horror. The figure in the distance was her, but it was wrong—distorted, darkened, like a reflection twisted in water.

The figure's eyes glowed with an eerie light, and as it drew closer, it spoke in a voice that was both her own and yet not:

"You think you can escape? You think you can change what was always meant to be?"

Veyrina felt the ground beneath her shift. The voice echoed in her mind, filling her with doubt, with fear. It was a reminder of the choices she had made, of the times she had failed, of the mistakes that haunted her.

Elyndra's hand gripped hers tighter, and she turned to face Veyrina. "Don't listen to it," she said, her voice firm but filled with the same uncertainty that Veyrina felt. "This is just another trick, another part of the echo."

But the echo—the twisted version of herself—continued, its words biting, sharp. "You cannot escape your fate. You cannot change the past. You are nothing but a reflection, doomed to repeat the cycle forever."

Veyrina's pulse quickened, and she felt the sting of the words cut into her. Doubt began to creep in, twisting around her thoughts. Was it true? Could they ever truly escape? Were they bound to this fate, to this eternal struggle, forever?

"Don't listen," Elyndra repeated, her voice insistent, pulling Veyrina's focus back to her. "We've already made our choice. We are together. That's all that matters."

But the voice, the twisted reflection of Veyrina, continued to mock her. "What if you made the wrong choice? What if you are destined to be alone again? What if the love you think you've found is only an illusion?"

Veyrina closed her eyes, trying to block out the voice. She could feel her breath coming faster, her heart pounding against her chest. She wanted to believe in their love. She wanted to believe that they could survive this, that they could break free. But the words continued to echo in her mind, gnawing at her, chipping away at her resolve.

"No," she whispered to herself. "I choose this. I choose her."

When she opened her eyes again, the figure had vanished, leaving only the oppressive silence of the barren world around them. Veyrina looked at Elyndra, who was watching her with a mix of concern and determination.

"We'll face this together," Veyrina said, her voice stronger now, the echo of doubt fading.

Elyndra nodded, her eyes soft but filled with the same resolve. "Together."

And as they stood there, side by side, a new realization dawned on Veyrina. The true trial had not been the realm, nor the labyrinth, nor the figure that had tried to tear them apart. The real trial was their ability to hold on to each other, to believe in the strength of their love despite everything the echo threw at them.

But the trial was far from over. The Unseen Realm was crumbling, but even as it did, the true cost of their sacrifice was only just beginning to unfold.

Sixteen

The Ruins of Time

The air around Veyrina and Elyndra hummed with a dissonant energy, as though the very fabric of reality was being pulled apart. The ground beneath them was no longer solid earth but an ever-shifting mix of jagged stone and ethereal light, a manifestation of the realm's unraveling. Their journey had brought them to this precipice—this place where every step they took could be their last.

"This is it," Elyndra whispered, her voice barely audible over the subtle, trembling vibration that seemed to rise from the core of the land. The weight of her words hung between them, thick with the enormity of what they were about to face. "We've come so far, Veyrina."

Veyrina's heart beat in sync with the pulse of the shifting world. Her eyes met Elyndra's, and for a moment, everything else seemed to fall away. Their hands brushed, fingers intertwining, and in that small, simple touch, they found the strength to keep moving forward. The end of their journey had come—whether it was their beginning or their undoing, they would find out soon enough.

Ahead of them lay the ruins—a labyrinth of crumbling towers, shattered columns, and half-submerged statues. Time itself seemed to have left its mark on this place. Everything about it screamed of abandonment, of centuries long past and forgotten civilizations. Yet, there was something alive in the silence. The ruins, though broken, held a strange kind of power—an ancient, dormant energy that whispered of secrets long buried.

Veyrina stepped forward, the ground beneath her feet shifting in response, as if the ruins were aware of her presence. She couldn't help but feel the weight of it all. The very air seemed to press against her chest, like a thousand eyes watching, waiting. This was the heart of the echo realm. The source of their torment. The origin of everything they had endured.

"This is where the echo began," Elyndra murmured, her voice filled with awe and trepidation. "These ruins… they're older than anything we've seen. Older than even the echo."

Veyrina nodded, but her mind was elsewhere. Her thoughts were consumed with the crystal—the key to severing the link between the echo and their world. The crystal they had heard of in stories, legends passed down in whispers from those who had come before them. Legends of the ancient power that could break the cycle. If they could find it, they could end this nightmare. But the cost of that power had never been clear.

As they ventured deeper into the ruins, the walls seemed to close in around them. The shadows grew thicker, more oppressive, as though the past itself was unwilling to let them move forward. Each step brought them closer to the heart of the ruins, but also closer to whatever force still guarded this place.

"There's something here," Veyrina whispered, pausing as the atmosphere grew heavier. The ground shifted again, this time with a strange, grinding sound—like something large, ancient, and unwilling to wake was stirring.

Before either of them could react, the air around them shifted. The shadows deepened, thickened, and from the darkness emerged the first of the guardians. A hulking figure, its body forged from the very stone of the ruins, moved toward them with a slow, deliberate pace. Its eyes glowed like embers, and its massive hands, each the size of a boulder, flexed as if preparing for battle.

"They're here," Elyndra muttered, her voice low and tense, as she drew her weapon from its sheath. The weapon glinted in the dim light, its edge sharp enough to cut through the fabric of time itself. "Ready yourself, Veyrina."

But Veyrina did not answer immediately. Her focus was elsewhere. She could feel it—a pull, deep within the ruins, as if the very structure of the place was reaching for them. She turned her head slowly, and in the distance, she saw it—the crystal.

It was a pale, ethereal object, floating above a pedestal at the center of the ruins. It pulsed with a soft, steady light, like the heartbeat of the realm itself. The sight of it filled her with a strange mix of hope and dread. They had found it. They had found the key to ending this torment. But it was guarded by more than just the stone figures. The air around the crystal shimmered with a strange energy, a force that she could feel clawing at her mind.

The guardians began to circle, their massive forms looming in the shadows. The first one took a step forward, its voice a low rumble that echoed through the ruins.

"Only those worthy may approach," it said, its voice ancient and unyielding. "Those who dare seek the crystal must face the trials of the heart."

Veyrina's grip on her weapon tightened. She could feel the force of the guardian's words resonating through the stone beneath her feet, vibrating in the marrow of her bones. She turned to Elyndra, her eyes filled with resolve.

"We have to make it through. Together," she said, her voice steady, despite the overwhelming odds.

Elyndra nodded, but her gaze was filled with uncertainty. "What if this is another test? What if we're meant to fail?"

"We won't," Veyrina said, her voice unyielding. "We've come too far. We won't let the echo win."

With that, the first guardian lunged, its massive hand swinging toward them with the force of a collapsing mountain. Veyrina ducked and rolled to the side, narrowly avoiding the blow. The air around them trembled, and the ground cracked open beneath their feet.

Elyndra was already in motion, her weapon flashing in the dim light. She struck, the blade meeting the guardian's stone arm with a resounding clang. But the guardian barely flinched. It swung again, this time faster, more vicious, and Elyndra barely managed to parry the blow, her knees buckling under the force.

"We can't fight them all at once," Veyrina called, her voice tinged with desperation. "There's too many."

The second guardian, smaller but equally as deadly, advanced from the other side. Veyrina's mind raced. They needed to reach the crystal. But they couldn't just walk past the guardians—they had to break through them.

"We have to distract them," Elyndra said, breathing hard as she parried another blow. "I'll take the left, you go for the right. We'll flank them."

Veyrina nodded, her pulse quickening. The plan was risky, but it was their only shot. As the guardians closed in on them, Veyrina charged, darting to the right, her feet barely touching the ground as she moved with a fluid grace. She struck first, aiming for the weakest point of the guardian's armor—its joints. The force of her strike sent a shockwave through the creature, and for a moment, it staggered, disoriented.

Elyndra took advantage of the opening, slashing at the second guardian with a flurry of blows. The air crackled with the sound of steel meeting stone, the force of their attack reverberating through the entire ruin.

But the guardians were relentless. They weren't just physical entities—they were the manifestation of the echo's will, designed to prevent anyone from reaching the heart of the ruin. They would stop at nothing to protect the crystal, to ensure that the cycle of the echo would continue.

"Veyrina, now!" Elyndra shouted, her voice strained as she held off the guardians' assault.

With a surge of adrenaline, Veyrina made a break for the crystal. She darted past the battling guardians, her heart pounding as she closed the distance. The crystal hovered before her, its light brighter now, calling to her. But as she reached out to touch it, a sudden, crushing force hit her from behind.

The first guardian had recovered, its stone hand closing around her ankle, dragging her backward.

"No!" Veyrina screamed, her voice raw with panic.

But before she could react, Elyndra was there. She dove toward the guardian, slashing with all her might. The blade found its mark, and with a deafening crack, the guardian shattered, its massive form crumbling to dust.

"Take it!" Elyndra cried, her voice fierce and desperate.

With trembling hands, Veyrina reached for the crystal, her fingers brushing its surface. The moment she touched it, a shockwave of energy surged through her, and the world around them seemed to shudder.

The echo was weakening. The realm was collapsing. They had done it.

But at what cost?

The crystal pulsed one final time, and the world around them fractured, splintering into a thousand pieces.

The ruins of time were no more. The echo's grip was slipping. But in the end, Veyrina and Elyndra were left with the choice they had feared.

The price of freedom had come.

The world around Veyrina and Elyndra continued to crumble as the echo, once a force that controlled every aspect of their existence, began to unravel. The ruins disintegrated into dust, the columns and stone structures falling away as though they had never existed. The ground beneath their feet shifted, collapsing into the chasm of nothingness.

Veyrina held the crystal in her trembling hands, its soft glow pulsing in rhythm with her racing heartbeat. She could feel its power surging through her veins, filling her with an overwhelming energy. But as the energy flowed into her, she also felt a cold emptiness creeping in—a sense that something was being torn away from her, something irreplaceable.

"What's happening?" Elyndra's voice was urgent, filled with panic as she looked around. She, too, felt the world fracturing. Her hand reached out to Veyrina, but the closer she got, the farther Veyrina seemed to move. It was as though an invisible wall had formed between them.

"The echo is falling apart," Veyrina gasped, her voice strained. "The crystal—it's doing something, but I can't hold it. It's too powerful."

Elyndra's eyes widened in understanding. She stepped closer, her gaze locking onto the crystal that Veyrina clutched. But as she moved, the space between them seemed to stretch, making it impossible for them to touch.

"The realm… It's collapsing. It won't hold us both," Veyrina whispered, the realization sinking into her soul like a stone. She could feel it, the weight of the choice that had always loomed over them but had never been so clear, so tangible.

The crystal was their salvation—but it demanded a sacrifice.

With a sickening clarity, Veyrina understood. One of them would have to remain behind, caught forever in the collapse of the echo. The other would be freed, but at what cost? The realm was breaking apart, and they had only one chance. One choice.

"No," Elyndra said, shaking her head fiercely, her voice breaking with the rawness of her emotion. "I won't let you do this. We can figure something out. We'll find a way together."

But Veyrina could already feel it—the weight of their shared past, the burden of the endless cycles that had brought them to this point. She felt it in every fiber of her being. If they both escaped, the cycle would simply begin again. The echo would return, stronger than ever.

"There's no other way, Elyndra," Veyrina said, her voice soft but filled with finality. "We can't both survive this. The crystal is only a momentary answer, but it demands a price. It's always been that way."

Elyndra's eyes were wide with disbelief, her expression stricken. She took another step toward Veyrina, her hands outstretched, but an invisible force held her back.

"I can't lose you. Not again," Elyndra whispered. Her voice was trembling, cracking under the strain. "Not after everything we've been through."

Tears pricked at the corners of Veyrina's eyes as she stepped back, clutching the crystal tightly against her chest. Her mind raced, but the answer was clear. She had seen the vision of the future, the endless loop of pain and longing, and the crystal was the only way to sever that connection. But to do so, one of them would have to remain in the echo for eternity.

"I love you, Elyndra," Veyrina said, her voice thick with emotion. "I always have. But I can't let this curse continue. I can't let the echo drag us through the same suffering, over and over."

The world around them seemed to shake violently as the echo's presence began to collapse entirely. The ruins had completely disintegrated, leaving them suspended in an empty void, a space between time and reality. And as the air around them grew thick with the power of the crystal, Veyrina realized that there was no more time to waste.

With a final glance at Elyndra, Veyrina raised the crystal, letting it glow even brighter in her hands. She could feel the pressure of the choice pressing down on her chest, suffocating her. But the crystal began to hum, vibrating with a raw, primal force that made her whole body tremble.

A wave of energy surged through her, and for a brief moment, everything stood still. She saw flashes—fragments of their shared history, their moments of love and loss, their fleeting joys and crushing heartbreaks. Their time together had been brief, but it had been everything.

Veyrina's heart clenched with love for Elyndra, but the realization was clear. For the echo to finally break, for the cycle to be severed once and for all, one of them would have to be lost. There was no other way.

The crystal pulsed with an intense light, and Veyrina felt the weight of it bearing down on her. She knew what she had to do. The pull was too strong. The connection between her and Elyndra was breaking, and she couldn't hold on any longer.

"I'm sorry," Veyrina whispered, her voice full of sorrow and love.

And then, with a final surge of energy, the crystal split open, unleashing a blinding wave of light. The energy engulfed her completely, and for a split second, everything went dark.

When Veyrina opened her eyes, the world around her was gone. The ruins, the void, the echo—it was all gone. She was alone.

She gasped for breath, her heart racing as she looked around. There was no sign of Elyndra. The empty space stretched infinitely before her, devoid of anything but a vast, endless silence.

"No," Veyrina breathed, her voice a desperate plea. "No, no, no…"

But the answer was already written in the fabric of the echo. The cycle was broken, the curse severed, but at the cost of everything.

Veyrina staggered backward, her heart sinking into the

depths of despair. She felt the weight of the sacrifice, the loss of her one true love, heavy on her soul. The price of breaking the curse had been too high, too unbearable.

Her body trembled with grief, her hands still clutching the remnants of the crystal. She could feel the echoes of their love, their bond, still lingering in the space around her. But Elyndra was gone. The one person who had shared this journey with her, the one person who had made all of this worth it—was lost.

And now, Veyrina was left alone in the fractured remnants of the echo realm. Her soul ached with the hollow emptiness of it all, the crushing weight of the truth that she had chosen to break the cycle, even if it meant losing everything she had ever wanted.

But the world beyond the echo would go on. She had made the ultimate sacrifice, and in doing so, had set the world free. For that, she could take some solace. But the pain of Elyndra's absence would be a constant reminder of the price she had paid.

The echo was broken, but it had claimed its due. And as Veyrina stood alone in the fractured world, she realized that the true cost of love and freedom was not something easily measured.

It was a price that would haunt her for eternity.

Seventeen

The Soul's Reckoning

The air was thick with the scent of burning time, as though every passing second had become something toxic, something that could not be undone. Veyrina's fingers gripped the crystal tighter, the power inside it humming in her palm like the beating of a heart that wasn't her own. Beside her, Elyndra stood still, the weight of the decision they had made pressing down on both of them.

In the silent expanse of the Unseen Realm, the two women stood facing the fading echo of their shared existence. The weight of their past, the gravity of the endless cycles, and the unbearable longing to be free from the curse of repeating lives—this was what had brought them here, to this moment.

Veyrina's breath came in sharp, shallow gasps, her heart thudding violently against her ribs. She knew what had to be done. They had come this far, only to be faced with the impossible choice of either staying within the endless loop of their cursed love or shattering it forever. The crystal was their final hope, their only chance to break free from the echo that had held them captive for so long.

But breaking the connection would not be without consequence.

Veyrina could feel the sharpness of Elyndra's gaze on her, the unspoken questions in the air between them. She could see the storm of emotions swirling in Elyndra's eyes—love, fear, determination. The bond they shared was palpable, and yet, despite their closeness, the space between them felt vast and insurmountable.

"Are you ready?" Elyndra's voice trembled as she asked the question, but there was a quiet strength in it as well.

Veyrina nodded, her gaze never leaving Elyndra. She wanted to tell her that everything would be fine, that they would both be okay. But the truth was, she didn't know.

"Together," she said, her voice steady despite the raging storm inside her.

Together. They would do this, no matter what.

The crystal in Veyrina's hand began to glow brighter, a fierce, blinding light that engulfed them both. And then, with a single breath, they broke the echo.

As the crystal's power surged, Veyrina felt a tearing sensation deep within her, a violent pull that split her soul in two. It was as though her very essence was being ripped apart, the pieces scattering to every corner of existence. Her body screamed with the weight of the moment, and she heard Elyndra's anguished cry beside her. But there was no time, no space to reach for each other as everything disintegrated around them.

The sound of cracking reality was deafening, and Veyrina's

vision blurred as an intense darkness swallowed them whole.

When Veyrina opened her eyes, the world was gone.

There were no stars, no sky, no solid ground beneath her. She was suspended in an endless void, a realm devoid of time, where nothing existed but the echo of her breath and the whispers of something ancient. A cold wind, sharp and bitter, brushed against her skin. And yet, there was no air, no tangible sense of anything at all, only the sensation of being lost.

She turned, searching for Elyndra, but the space around her stretched out in all directions. There was no one here, no one but her. The ache in her chest deepened, the weight of her own isolation settling like a heavy cloak.

"Elyndra?" Her voice cracked as she called out, the sound lost in the empty expanse.

The silence that followed was oppressive, thick enough to choke on. She swallowed, desperate to find her footing, to make sense of the emptiness. And then, as if the very fabric of the void responded to her despair, a figure materialized before her.

It was Elyndra, but it was not Elyndra.

The form standing before her was a twisted reflection of the woman she loved. Her hair, once soft and flowing, was now tangled and dark, her eyes vacant pools of blackness, devoid of recognition. The figure wore a strange expression—an eerie, knowing smile that didn't belong to the Elyndra she knew.

"You think you can escape," the figure said, its voice low, hollow. "You think you've broken free. But the price of your love was never so simple."

Veyrina stepped back, fear creeping up her spine as she took in the sight of the thing before her. It wasn't Elyndra. It was something else—something twisted, something made of the very echo they had tried to destroy.

The figure raised a hand, and in an instant, the void around them began to shift, warping into something far darker. The shadows grew thick and alive, pulling at Veyrina's limbs, threatening to drag her into a chasm of eternal darkness.

"You've set it all in motion," the figure hissed. "The forgotten gods will have their reckoning. And your souls will pay the price for your defiance."

Before Veyrina could react, the figure lunged forward, and everything went black.

Veyrina awoke with a start, gasping for breath. Her heart pounded violently in her chest, and she blinked rapidly, struggling to make sense of her surroundings. She was no longer in the void. Instead, she found herself standing in an unfamiliar land—a barren wasteland, where the sky was perpetually dimmed by a veil of thick clouds. The ground beneath her was cracked and dry, as though no life had ever touched it.

And yet, she felt a presence—a pull—an undeniable weight at the back of her mind. She wasn't alone.

"Elyndra?" she called out, her voice hoarse and trembling.

At first, there was no answer. But then, from the distance, a figure emerged from the haze.

It was Elyndra. She was standing there, in the same barren landscape, as though she had been waiting for Veyrina to come to her. But something was different about her now. Her eyes were clouded, distant, as though she no longer remembered the woman who stood before her.

"Elyndra?" Veyrina repeated, her voice more desperate now.

The figure turned slowly, her expression unreadable. "You think you can hold onto me," she said, her voice sounding distant, as though it came from far away. "But we're not the same anymore. The sacrifice is ours, Veyrina. The gods will take what they are owed."

A chill ran down Veyrina's spine as she realized that the woman in front of her was not the Elyndra she knew. She was different—changed—twisted by the very forces they had tried to defy.

"You were warned," the figure continued. "The price of love is never paid in simple ways."

The earth beneath them trembled, and Veyrina staggered, struggling to maintain her balance. The land around them seemed to shift and twist, as though time itself was unspooling, unraveling everything they had worked to build.

"You've broken the cycle," the figure said with a hollow laugh. "But you cannot escape the gods' judgment. They will make sure you remember the price of your rebellion."

The ground cracked open beneath them, and Veyrina felt herself falling, plunging into a dark abyss where memories collided—faded images of lives they had lived and lost, of endless love and endless betrayal. She reached out, calling for Elyndra, but the figure was already gone, lost to the swirling darkness.

And then, as the darkness closed in around her, she realized the truth. The echo wasn't simply a force—they were its creation. Their love had been a part of the echo's cycle, an endless dance of fate. And now, as the gods of time and memory watched, they would make their final reckoning.

Veyrina's soul screamed in agony as the realization set in. This wasn't just about breaking the curse. It was about surviving the consequences. The wrath of the forgotten gods was upon them.

And there was nowhere to hide.

Veyrina's world blurred, the memories of past lives slipping like water through her fingers, each one becoming more distant, more ethereal. As she fell deeper into the abyss, the familiar warmth of Elyndra's presence began to fade, replaced by an unsettling chill that clawed at her chest.

She reached out, her fingers trembling, desperate for some connection, some reminder of what had once been. Her heart ached with the weight of all the lost moments, the endless cycles of love and pain, of regret and yearning.

Where was Elyndra?

The question echoed through her mind like a haunting refrain, but no answer came. The void swallowed it whole.

Then, with a sudden jolt, the fall stopped. She landed softly, as though the very fabric of time itself had caught her in its embrace. Veyrina blinked, her senses reeling as she pushed herself up from the ground.

The landscape around her was barren—dead trees twisted into unnatural shapes, their branches like gnarled fingers reaching up to the ashen sky. The ground was cracked and scorched, devoid of life. A cold, oppressive silence hung in the air, as though nothing had moved for eons.

And yet, something was there.

In the distance, a figure stood, bathed in an eerie, shimmering light. It was Elyndra—or at least, it resembled her. But the woman standing before Veyrina was a distorted reflection of the one she loved. Elyndra's features were sharp, almost hollow, her eyes an unnatural, glowing silver. She was encased in an ethereal, shifting mist, her form flickering like a ghost trapped in the mortal world.

Veyrina's breath caught in her throat as she took a step forward, her voice trembling. "Elyndra…"

The figure looked up, its eyes—those familiar, haunting eyes—fixed on her. But there was no recognition in them. Instead, there was an unsettling emptiness, as though the woman she had once known no longer existed.

"You think you can break the cycle," Elyndra's voice echoed, but it was warped, a hollow distortion of the love they had shared. "But you have made a terrible mistake."

"No," Veyrina whispered, stepping forward again. "I had to do this. I had to break the echo. We had to be free."

The figure smiled, but it was not the warm, comforting smile that Veyrina remembered. It was cold, twisted, a mockery of the love they had once shared. "You thought you could escape," it said softly, "but the gods of time do not forgive. They will claim what is theirs."

The words sent a chill through Veyrina's spine, and her heart clenched in fear. The figure before her shifted, moving like a shadow through the fog, its form flickering with every step. As it approached, the ground beneath Veyrina began to tremble, and the once-still air began to vibrate with an ancient energy.

"You are caught in the web of time," the figure continued, its voice rising in intensity. "Every choice you make, every action, only weaves you deeper into the fabric of fate. You can never escape the gods' judgment. They will reclaim what you have stolen."

Terror rose in Veyrina's chest as she realized the gravity of the situation. The gods—those ancient, forgotten entities that controlled the threads of time—had been watching them. They were the ones who had twisted their lives, weaving them into an endless cycle of love, loss, and heartbreak.

And now, they were ready to take back what had been taken from them.

But even as fear clawed at her, something deep within Veyrina refused to submit. She couldn't—she wouldn't—let this be the end.

"No!" she cried, her voice raw with desperation. "We chose this! We chose to break the echo, to defy fate!"

The figure's smile faltered, and for a brief moment, something like a flicker of recognition crossed its face. But it was fleeting, a mere shadow of the woman Elyndra had once been.

"You think your love is enough?" the figure asked, its voice softening, almost mournful. "The gods will not be moved by your defiance. They have seen your love. They have seen your pain. But your souls belong to them now. There is no escape."

Veyrina's pulse raced as the figure raised a hand toward her. A cold wind whipped through the barren landscape, and the sky above darkened, the clouds swirling like a storm had gathered in the very fabric of time. The air grew heavy, thick with the weight of a thousand years, a thousand broken promises.

And then, the ground beneath her feet cracked open.

Veyrina stumbled back, gasping as a deep chasm formed before her, the darkness yawning wide and threatening to swallow her whole. The crack in the earth pulsed with an eerie, otherworldly light, and from it, something began to emerge.

It was an entity—an ancient, towering being whose form seemed to be made of the very fabric of time itself. Its body shifted, morphing with each passing second, its shape never fully solidifying, as though it were made from the very essence of the echo. Its eyes were twin orbs of dark light, filled with the weight of millennia, ancient and full of wrath.

The figure before her—Elyndra's twisted form—stepped aside, as if bowing before the entity. "The gods have come to collect," it said, its voice like a whisper in the wind. "Your defiance has brought forth their reckoning."

Veyrina's heart pounded in her chest as the figure advanced, its presence suffocating, a shadow that stretched across the very air she breathed.

The world trembled as the towering entity raised its arm, and the ground beneath them seemed to crack open even further, deepening the rift between them and everything they had known. "You are to be judged," the entity's voice thundered. "The cycle cannot be broken. Your souls are bound to the echo, and the gods will reclaim what they are owed."

"No!" Veyrina cried, her voice rising in desperation. "I won't let you take her. I won't let you take us!"

The words were no sooner out of her mouth than a violent pulse of energy shot through her, knocking her backward. The force of it was like a slap from the very hands of time, sending her sprawling onto the ground.

For a moment, the world spun, the weight of the entity's power pressing down on her. She gasped for air, her body trembling, her mind reeling from the sheer force of the magic that surrounded them. She could feel the pull of the echo, the remnants of all their past lives, crashing over her in waves.

And yet, in the midst of it all, she felt a flicker—something that could not be extinguished.

Elyndra.

Even though she stood before her in this twisted form, even though the gods had come to claim their due, Veyrina's heart refused to let go. She reached out, extending her hand toward the woman she loved, toward the woman who had once shared her soul.

"Elyndra," she whispered, her voice breaking. "I won't leave you. Not now. Not ever."

There was no response at first. But then, slowly, Elyndra's twisted form began to flicker, her eyes shifting between recognition and emptiness. She took a single step toward Veyrina, her hand outstretched.

The world trembled again.

The sky above seemed to crack, the very heavens themselves on the brink of unraveling. Time itself groaned under the strain, and Veyrina felt her soul teetering on the edge of annihilation.

"Do not test us further," the entity warned, its voice deep and thunderous. "The gods will have their price."

But Veyrina did not look away from Elyndra. She could feel the pull of their connection, stronger than any force that sought to separate them. And in that moment, she knew what she had to do.

Even if it meant everything.

"I love you," she whispered, her heart breaking with the weight of it all.

And with that, the very fabric of time began to unravel.

Eighteen

The Return of the Echo

The sky overhead trembled, a low rumble of thunder that seemed to emanate from the very bones of the world. The air crackled with tension, thick and heavy, pressing down on Veyrina's chest, making it difficult to breathe. The land around them was shifting, the ground beneath her feet warping and undulating, as though the very fabric of existence was coming undone.

Elyndra stood beside her, their hands brushing in a fleeting moment of contact that sent a spark of warmth between them, though it was rapidly fading. The two women locked eyes, the bond between them pulsating like a heartbeat, but even that felt uncertain, as if it might slip away into the ether at any moment.

The veil between the realms—the thin boundary that had held the echo at bay—was tearing apart. The world around them was unraveling, as though time itself had grown too weak to hold the threads of the universe together.

Veyrina's stomach churned. The destruction was not a simple fading of reality, a mere dissolution into nothingness. No, this was something far more profound. The echoes of their pasts—of lives lived and loved, of mistakes and regrets—surged back like a tidal wave, crashing into their minds with violent force. The air itself seemed to scream with the weight of them.

Then, a low, guttural laugh echoed from the shadows.

Veyrina turned sharply, her heart racing. The figure that emerged from the darkness was tall, a towering wraith whose eyes glowed with an unearthly light, cold and malevolent. His form flickered between solid and spectral, his body shifting in and out of existence like a phantom caught between worlds. He was a god—a forgotten one, bound by the very laws of time and space, now risen from the depths of the echo to claim what was his.

Ithranos Melaes.

The spirit of vengeance.

His voice slithered through the air, reverberating in the depths of their souls. "You have tampered with forces beyond your understanding," he sneered, his tone full of ancient malice. "The gods will reclaim what you have stolen, and you will be nothing but echoes in the wind."

The very land seemed to groan in response to his words, the sky above darkening further as if in mourning for the unraveling of the realms. The ground split open beneath their feet, jagged fissures tearing through the earth, sending tremors through the air.

Veyrina's pulse quickened. She could feel the weight of the gods' anger pressing down on her, the sheer force of their power shaking the world to its core.

Elyndra's hand tightened around hers, her voice a whisper of resolve. "We have come this far, Veyrina. We cannot turn back now. We have to fight."

But the world was no longer a place for fighting with swords or magic. There were no weapons to draw, no spells to cast—only the unrelenting power of their bond and the echoes of the past, both of which were now being ripped apart by the furious wrath of the gods.

The wraith stepped forward, his presence overwhelming. "Your love is nothing," he said, his voice like ice scraping across stone. "It is but a fleeting illusion. The echo will devour you both, and your love will be nothing but ashes in the wind."

A great blast of energy surged from him, sending a shockwave of darkness rippling outward. Veyrina stumbled back, her body trembling under the force of the attack. She gripped Elyndra's hand tighter, refusing to let go. The world around them was spiraling, collapsing, and yet the warmth of Elyndra's touch was the only thing that held her steady.

"We cannot defeat him with strength alone," Veyrina whispered, her voice full of fear and determination. "We need to believe in each other."

Elyndra's eyes softened, and for a moment, the tumult around them seemed to fade into the background. In the midst of the chaos, there was only the two of them—their bond, their love. And that, Veyrina knew, was their true strength.

But the gods were not so easily silenced.

With a cry of fury, Ithranos Melaes raised his arms, his body crackling with dark energy. The ground split wider, and the air became thick with the weight of ancient power, as though the very forces of creation were being undone.

From the cracks in the earth, dark tendrils of energy lashed out, wrapping around them both, trying to pull them into the depths of the echo. Veyrina's heart pounded as the tendrils tightened, their cold fingers sinking into her flesh, dragging her toward the abyss.

And yet, through the suffocating darkness, she could still feel Elyndra beside her. Their connection remained strong, an unbreakable thread that tethered them to one another, even as the world crumbled around them.

We cannot be separated. We are stronger than this.

Veyrina's thoughts burned through the darkness like a beacon of light. She squeezed Elyndra's hand, and together, they began to pull against the tendrils, fighting with everything they had left. The air around them crackled with energy, and the world seemed to hold its breath, waiting for what would come next.

The wraith sneered, his form flickering with dark laughter. "Your love is nothing against the gods. It is a child's dream, and it will die here, with you."

But Veyrina's resolve was unshakable. She lifted her chin, her gaze meeting Elyndra's. Their eyes locked, and in that moment, there was no more fear, no more doubt. There was only trust—trust in each other, trust in the love they had fought for, fought through countless lifetimes to protect.

"We will not be your slaves," Veyrina said, her voice rising with defiance. "Our love is our strength. And we will not let it be taken."

Together, they reached for the heart of their connection, the source of their love, the very soul of who they were. The energy around them intensified, the world itself seeming to recoil from the force of their determination.

And then, with a final cry, they unleashed their love.

The tendrils of darkness recoiled, shuddering as if in pain, and the wraith let out a guttural scream of rage. The very air seemed to bend and twist, the echo itself recoiling, as though it could not withstand the force of their bond.

The ground beneath them shook violently, the chasm widening further as if the realm itself was ripping apart. But still, the light of their love shone brighter, pushing back the darkness, forcing the echo to recede.

The wraith's form flickered, his eyes filled with hate and fear. "You think you have won?" he hissed. "The gods will never forget what you have taken."

But Veyrina and Elyndra did not flinch. They stood firm, their hands clasped tightly, their hearts beating in unison. Their love was a force of nature, stronger than any god, stronger than any echo. And in that moment, they knew they had won.

With a final, resounding crack, the realm collapsed around them. The sky shattered, the earth split open, and the wraith was torn from existence, his dark form dissipating into nothingness. The gods' power—their fury—was gone, shattered by the sheer will of their love.

But even as the echo faded, the world was not yet whole. There was still a price to be paid. The realm had crumbled, the fabric of time itself torn apart. Veyrina and Elyndra stood amidst the ruins, their bodies battered, their souls spent, but their bond unbroken.

"We did it," Elyndra whispered, her voice barely audible, her eyes filled with both relief and sorrow.

Veyrina nodded, her hand still tightly clutching Elyndra's. "But at what cost?"

The question hung in the air, unspoken but understood. The echo had been vanquished, the gods defeated, but the realm was still unraveling. There was still one final battle to fight—the battle for their future, and the price of love in a world where time had been broken.

As Veyrina and Elyndra stood amidst the ruins, the air thick with the scent of destruction and the remnants of ancient magic, the world around them seemed to pulse in fractured silence. The sky above had lost its color, no longer vibrant, but a ghostly shade of gray that bled into the jagged horizon. The echoes of their pasts had faded, but the remnants of those memories still lingered, clawing at the edges of their consciousness like shadows in the periphery of their vision.

The ground beneath them was cracked, split open like a wound that refused to heal. A cold wind whipped through the remnants of the realm, sending dust swirling around them in eerie spirals. The realm, once a vibrant and ever-shifting tapestry, was now a wasteland—a broken reflection of the world they had fought to preserve.

Veyrina looked to Elyndra, their eyes meeting in a shared understanding, a momentary flash of connection amidst the chaos. But it was fleeting. There was something deeper now—a presence that hung heavy in the air. The energy that had once bound the realms was gone, replaced by a crushing silence, an emptiness that spread like poison through the very fabric of the world.

"We've won," Elyndra whispered, her voice hoarse, yet firm. "But it feels as though we've lost everything."

Veyrina swallowed hard, the weight of the words settling heavily in her chest. They had succeeded in breaking the cycle of the echo, severing their connection to the gods and to the dark forces that had ruled the realm. But what had they truly won? The world around them was collapsing, crumbling into dust, and with it, the memories that had bound them together for centuries. Their love was strong, but in the wake of the battle, it was no longer enough to keep the pieces of their world from falling apart.

They had destroyed the echo, but at what cost?

A sharp pang of loss gnawed at Veyrina's heart, and she could feel it mirrored in Elyndra's presence, their souls still intertwined despite the unraveling of everything they had known. She reached for Elyndra's hand, their fingers intertwining once more, the contact grounding her amidst the swirling chaos.

"I don't know what we've sacrificed, but I know one thing," Veyrina said, her voice steady despite the turmoil around them. "We still have each other. Even if everything else is gone, we have this."

Elyndra nodded, her grip tightening. "But how long can we hold onto that?" She looked around at the destruction, her gaze haunted. "This world—it's not the same. It's falling apart."

Veyrina's chest tightened as she turned her eyes toward the horizon. She could see the edges of the realm beginning to peel away, the very foundation of reality coming undone. The ruins of the once-mighty structure they stood upon were now nothing more than broken stones, scattered remnants of a civilization lost to time.

"You're right," Veyrina murmured, the truth of Elyndra's words settling in her gut like a cold stone. "The world is unraveling, but we can't let go. We can't let the sacrifice be for nothing."

The wind howled through the wreckage, carrying with it

the faintest echo of the gods' vengeful whispers. The spirit of Ithranos Melaes had been vanquished, but the consequences of their actions were far from over. The fabric of the realms was torn, and the destruction was far from complete.

"Is this it, then?" Elyndra asked, her voice trembling with the weight of the question. "Are we to fade into nothingness?"

Veyrina could see the fear in Elyndra's eyes, the same fear that had plagued her own heart since they had first stepped into this realm. But this time, it was different. There was no escape, no easy path forward. Only the uncertain, dark future they now faced.

"I don't know," Veyrina admitted, her voice soft with uncertainty. "But I do know that we can't give up. We still have the crystal. We still have a chance to rebuild. We can find a way to mend the broken pieces. We have to."

Elyndra looked down at their intertwined hands, her expression softening. "I can't imagine a world without you, Veyrina. After everything we've been through... I don't want to let go."

The words hung heavy in the air between them, a promise and a plea all at once. Veyrina's heart tightened as she leaned in, pressing her forehead to Elyndra's.

"We won't let go," Veyrina whispered. "Not yet. Not ever."

But as they stood together, in the heart of the crumbling realm, a new presence emerged from the shadows. A low hum filled the air, a sound that seemed to pulse with the rhythm of the world itself. Veyrina's senses sharpened, and she turned, her pulse quickening as the shape materialized before them.

It was a figure cloaked in shadow, its form indistinct, flickering in and out of reality like a specter. But as it drew closer, the outline became clearer—an ancient being, its face hidden in the folds of its cloak, but its presence unmistakable.

The forgotten god.

"I see you," the being intoned, its voice a deep, resonating sound that echoed through the very core of the realm. "You have defied us. Broken the cycle. Destroyed the echo."

Veyrina and Elyndra exchanged a glance, both of them stiffening. They had thought the gods were gone—vanquished in the battle with Ithranos Melaes. But here, before them, was yet another force of the realm. Another god.

The being's eyes—if they could be called eyes—glowed with an ancient, terrible light, the depth of time itself reflected in its gaze.

"You think you have won?" the god continued, its voice like the rumble of an impending storm. "You have only begun to understand the true cost of your actions."

Veyrina stood taller, her heart pounding as she faced the god. "What do you want from us?" she demanded, the words sharp and defiant. "We've done what you asked. We broke the echo. We destroyed the wraith. What more do you want?"

The being tilted its head, as if considering her words. "You have shattered the link to the echo. But in doing so, you have severed the bond that holds this realm together. You have broken time itself."

Elyndra's breath caught in her throat. "What are you saying?"

The god's gaze pierced them both. "I am the keeper of the threads of time. I hold the balance between the realms. You have disrupted that balance, and now, everything is unraveling. There is no returning from this."

Veyrina's blood ran cold. She had known the cost of their actions, but she hadn't known the full extent of it—the very fabric of time was crumbling because of their choice. Their love had come at a terrible price.

"Is there no way to undo this?" Elyndra asked, her voice trembling.

The god's lips parted, a sound that could have been a laugh—or a lament. "There is a way. But it is a path none have dared walk. You must choose—restore the realm, or let it fall. The cost is more than either of you can bear."

The god's eyes narrowed, and the air around them thickened with the weight of its words. "If you choose to restore the realm, you will have to sacrifice everything. Your memories. Your love. Your very souls."

Veyrina's heart skipped a beat. She turned to Elyndra, her face pale with shock. The decision had never been so dire.

"Do you hear that?" the god's voice crooned. "You will lose each other, lose everything you are, if you choose to save this broken world. Your love, your bond, will be gone forever. So I ask you now, before you make your decision—will you sacrifice your love to restore what you've destroyed?"

The silence stretched between them, thick and heavy, as the two women stood on the precipice of an impossible choice.

And in that moment, Veyrina knew one thing for sure:

No matter what the cost, no matter how deep the sacrifice, she would never let go of Elyndra.

But the world had a price—and time itself was no exception.

Nineteen

The End of Time

The world was crumbling.

Veyrina and Elyndra stood at the epicenter of the unraveling realm, the ground beneath their feet fractured and splintering like glass under a weight too immense to bear. The once-vibrant skies had turned to a swirling vortex of darkness, tendrils of shadow reaching out from the very fabric of existence itself, tearing it apart. The air crackled with a raw energy—raw and primal—whispering with the echoes of forgotten gods and lost lives, their voices reverberating through time like a haunting symphony.

"Do you hear it?" Elyndra whispered, her voice barely audible over the growing roar of chaos around them. Her hand tightened around Veyrina's, and in that touch, Veyrina felt the tremor of Elyndra's pulse, fast and erratic, as if the very beat of her heart was caught in the collapse of the world itself.

Veyrina nodded, her chest heavy with the weight of it all—

the weight of the decisions they had made, the sacrifices they had already given, and the future that now hung in the balance. The echo of their past lives reverberated through the very core of her being. Faces and voices long forgotten surged to the forefront of her mind, memories fragmented, scattered like shards of glass.

They were surrounded by the voices of their ancestors, their past selves. They could hear their laughter, their cries, their joys and their pains, all overlapping and blending into one overwhelming chorus. Their past lives called to them, the words impossible to discern, but the emotion—raw and pure—was unmistakable. It was the collective weight of all they had ever been, all they had ever loved.

"Veyrina," Elyndra said, her breath catching in her throat. "What if we can't fix this? What if everything we've done… what if it's all for nothing?"

Veyrina turned to her, seeing the fear that mirrored her own. It was a fear they had never allowed to show, a fear they had buried beneath their love, beneath their fight to break the echo's curse. But now, with the realm disintegrating around them, it was impossible to ignore.

"We can't give up," Veyrina said, her voice strong, though every part of her wanted to crumble under the weight of the destruction. "We've come too far. We've fought too hard. There has to be a way."

But the silence that followed her words was deafening. The echoes of their past lives pulsed, growing louder and louder, until it felt like the very foundation of their existence was trembling, threatening to collapse beneath the strain. Their love, their connection—was it enough?

Suddenly, the ground beneath their feet gave way, plunging

them into the abyss.

For a moment, there was nothing but darkness—black, suffocating, and cold. Time itself seemed to stretch and warp, leaving them suspended in a void between moments, between breaths, between life and death.

And then—light.

It wasn't the gentle glow of dawn, nor the fiery blaze of the sun. It was something else entirely—a blinding brilliance, too pure and too powerful to comprehend. It surged through them, through their veins, through their hearts, until they felt as if they were being torn apart and remade in the same instant.

"Elyndra!" Veyrina cried out, reaching for her in the suffocating light. Her voice was drowned out by the sound of rushing wind and the roar of crashing waves.

"I'm here!" Elyndra's voice was a lifeline, pulling Veyrina back from the brink of madness. Their hands found each other, their fingers interlacing tightly as they struggled to hold on to one another amidst the blinding chaos.

They were no longer in the realm they had fought so hard to preserve. They were somewhere else—somewhere beyond time itself.

The light faded, leaving them standing at the center of a vast, empty space. There was no sky, no ground, no stars. Just a void—a gaping, infinite chasm that stretched out in every direction, as far as the eye could see.

"Where are we?" Elyndra's voice trembled, and Veyrina could hear the same fear that had gripped her before, now rising in Elyndra's voice like a tangible force.

"We're… between worlds," Veyrina whispered, her gaze flicking around, searching for something—anything—that might offer them answers. But there was nothing. Only the vast emptiness.

Suddenly, a voice—low and ancient, echoing through the void—spoke. "You have come far. Too far, perhaps."

Veyrina and Elyndra spun, searching for the source of the voice, but the darkness swallowed them whole. It was everywhere, and yet nowhere at all.

"Who are you?" Veyrina demanded, her heart pounding in her chest.

"I am the Keeper of the Threshold," the voice replied, each word reverberating in their bones. "I am the one who guards the boundary between the realms. You have crossed it, and in doing so, you have shattered the balance that once held the fabric of time together."

Elyndra's grip on Veyrina's hand tightened, her knuckles pale. "What do we do? How do we fix this?"

"You cannot fix it," the voice answered, its tone sorrowful. "Time, once broken, cannot be mended."

A cold, suffocating silence filled the void, and for a moment, neither of them spoke. Veyrina could feel her heart beating in her chest, slow and steady, as the weight of the voice's words settled in.

"There is a way," the voice continued, its tone heavy. "But it requires a sacrifice—a final act of true unity, one that binds your souls together in a way that will erase the past and allow the future to begin anew."

Veyrina's breath caught in her throat. "What kind of sacrifice?"

"The kind that will erase everything you have ever known. Your memories. Your love. The very essence of who you are."

Elyndra's eyes widened in horror. "You're asking us to give up everything?"

The voice was silent for a long moment before it spoke again, its words filled with sorrow. "You have fought to break the cycle, to restore the balance. But to do so, you must give up your past. You must merge your souls, willingly, to restore time and allow the world to begin again. You will no longer remember who you were, or the love you shared. But your love will live on, in another time, another place."

Veyrina felt her heart shatter, the weight of the decision pressing down on her with an unbearable force. The choice seemed impossible.

"Is there no other way?" Elyndra asked, her voice trembling.

"There is no other way," the voice replied, its tone heavy with finality. "Time must be restored. The echo must be severed completely. To heal the realm, to ensure the future, you must merge as one."

Veyrina turned to Elyndra, her heart aching with a love so deep it threatened to consume her. She could feel Elyndra's warmth, her presence, the bond they shared—stronger than any force in the universe. But to give it up, to erase everything they had fought for… was it worth it?

Elyndra's eyes searched hers, the fear in them giving way to something else—a quiet understanding. "We've already lost so much. But if this is the price of saving the world, then we have no choice."

Tears welled in Veyrina's eyes as she nodded. "I will never forget you, Elyndra. No matter what happens."

Elyndra smiled softly, the expression bittersweet. "I will never forget you, either. No matter where time takes us."

Together, they stepped forward, their hands still clasped tightly, as they embraced the final sacrifice. The void around them began to swirl, the air crackling with energy as their souls intertwined. The past, the present, and the future converged into a single point—a moment that would stretch out for eternity.

And as they merged, their love became the cornerstone of time itself.

The echo of their souls, once fragmented and lost, now united in a single, unbreakable bond. The realm began to heal, slowly at first, then faster, as if the very fabric of reality had been restored. The collapsing world stabilized, the cracks mending themselves as time resumed its flow.

But as the light dimmed and the world began to take shape around them once more, Veyrina and Elyndra found themselves standing in a new place—a place they didn't recognize. The past was gone, the echo faded into nothingness, and their love was now a powerful force that transcended time.

They stood on the threshold of a new world, free from the curse of the echo, free to choose their destiny.

Together.

And for the first time, time itself felt like a gift.

The world around them pulsed as the last remnants of the echo faded into the ether. The realm—this strange, timeless place— began to shift. The darkness that had engulfed everything was beginning to give way to something new, something tangible, but unfamiliar. Veyrina and Elyndra stood amidst this transformation, their bodies trembling with the weight of what they had just done. They had given everything, their pasts, their memories, and now… their love was all that remained.

In the distance, a glimmer of light began to appear, faint at first, like the first rays of dawn breaking through the darkest night. The light spread slowly, pushing back the shadows, revealing a land that neither of them recognized. They stood on the edge of a vast, open field, the grass swaying gently in a breeze that seemed to carry the scent of earth, salt, and something ancient, like the air of a forgotten world.

"What is this place?" Elyndra whispered, her voice full of awe and confusion. She reached out, touching the grass beneath her feet as if it might disappear the moment she let go. It felt real. Solid. Alive.

"I don't know," Veyrina murmured, her gaze sweeping the horizon. The world seemed suspended between moments, as if time itself hadn't quite made its way here yet. The air was thick with the sensation of something unfinished, something about to begin.

Together, they stepped forward, the weight of the decision still settling over them. There was no turning back. Their souls had merged, the final act of sacrifice that restored the balance, but it had come at the cost of everything they had known. The memories that had once defined them—of love, of battles fought, of lives lived—were slipping through their fingers like sand.

Veyrina looked at Elyndra, the familiar warmth of her presence still a constant. Despite the loss of their past, the bond between them remained, undeniable and unbroken. She could still feel the echo of Elyndra's heart beating, synchronized with her own. It was as if their love had transcended the boundaries of time and space. No curse, no force, no power could sever it.

"Do you remember… anything?" Elyndra asked, her voice soft but desperate. The fear in her eyes was impossible to ignore, though she tried to mask it with a flicker of hope.

Veyrina closed her eyes for a moment, as if to sift through the fragments of their past that remained. There were flashes—

fragments of memories like distant stars twinkling in the vast, endless night. She saw the soft touch of Elyndra's hand, the warmth of their shared laughter, the joy of moments they had lived and lost.

But none of it felt complete. None of it was clear.

"I… I remember you," Veyrina said, her voice thick with emotion. "I remember *us*."

Elyndra's breath hitched, and she took a step forward, her fingers brushing Veyrina's cheek, her touch tender, as if she was afraid the moment might disappear if she didn't hold on tightly. "Then, that's enough."

"But is it?" Veyrina replied, her voice barely a whisper, her heart aching with the weight of her own uncertainty. "We've lost so much. Will we ever find our way back?"

Elyndra paused, her gaze intense, searching Veyrina's face. "I don't know what the future holds for us, but I know one thing. As long as we have each other, nothing else matters. We'll forge a new path, even if we have to make it from nothing."

The ground beneath them trembled slightly, the world shaking as if it were still adjusting to the shift. The light around them grew brighter, warmer, and Veyrina felt a strange sense of clarity wash over her. She could feel the faint stirrings of time moving again, slow at first, then gradually speeding up. The world was being reborn—reformed. This land they had found was new, untouched by the forces that had threatened to tear everything apart.

A sound broke the silence—low and rumbling, like distant thunder, but filled with an energy that made the air itself vibrate. The light around them dimmed for a moment before flaring once more, revealing a figure emerging from the darkness. It was neither human nor god, but something in between. Its form was constantly shifting, fluid, like smoke caught in a breeze. Its eyes—golden, ancient—gleamed with an unnatural intelligence.

The figure spoke, its voice like a low hum, vibrating through the very core of Veyrina and Elyndra's beings. "You have succeeded… but the balance is delicate. The price of your sacrifice is great, but your bond—your love—it has changed everything. You have defied the will of the forgotten gods, the forces of fate. For that, you must be tested once more."

"What do you want from us now?" Elyndra asked, her voice steady despite the growing unease. She stood firm beside Veyrina, their hands still clasped tightly together.

The figure shifted closer, its presence filling the space, overwhelming their senses. "You must prove that your love is enough to sustain the world you have saved. The gods you defied will not rest. The echoes of your past will return, seeking vengeance, seeking to reclaim the power they lost. To prevent the world from slipping back into the chaos from which it was born, you must stand together. You must face the gods, face the consequences of your choices."

Veyrina's heart raced as the figure's words settled over her like a cold wave. The gods—they had been the architects of the curse that had bound them. Now, with everything at stake, they would return, their wrath unforgiving.

"What do you mean—face the gods?" Veyrina demanded, her pulse quickening. "How can we fight gods? What can we do?"

"You will not fight with weapons or magic," the figure answered, its golden eyes shimmering with unspoken knowledge. "You will fight with the strength of your love. Only by proving that your bond is true, unwavering, can you ensure that the balance remains. The gods will test you—not just as lovers, but as souls bound together by a power greater than the gods themselves. The choice is yours. Will you face the wrath of the forgotten gods, or will you let the world fall back into chaos?"

Elyndra's grip tightened on Veyrina's hand, her voice fierce despite the uncertainty. "We will face them. Together."

The figure nodded, as if expecting nothing less. "Then the test begins."

With a sudden surge of energy, the ground beneath them shifted again. The world rippled, as if reality itself was distorting, pulling them into another realm—another test. The scene around them twisted, revealing a darkened sky filled with swirling clouds, lightning cracking through the air. The land around them was barren, cracked earth stretching out in every direction. A sense of ancient, untold power lingered in the air, as if they were standing at the very edge of existence itself.

And then, they appeared.

The forgotten gods.

A chorus of ethereal, godlike beings—cloaked in shadows, their eyes glowing with unearthly fire. Their voices echoed like thunder, resonating through the fabric of time. "You dare defy us, mortals? You dare to rewrite the fate we have crafted?"

Veyrina's heart hammered in her chest, but she stood tall, her gaze unwavering. "We defied you because our love is stronger than any fate you could impose. We chose each other, no matter the cost. And we will fight to protect the world we have saved."

The gods laughed, their voices dark and booming. "Foolish. You are nothing more than sparks in the vast sea of time. But we will give you your test. We will see if your love is truly strong enough to withstand what we will throw at you."

The world around them began to shift once more, the gods' wrath descending in a wave of overwhelming force. Veyrina and Elyndra stood together, ready for the test, knowing that their love was the only weapon they had.

Their bond, unbroken, would be the key to saving this world—and ensuring their love was never lost again.

And so, with the gods circling them like predators, the final battle for the realm began.

Twenty

Echoes of Forever

The air was thick with the weight of the decision they had made, yet, as Veyrina and Elyndra stood together, hands entwined, a sense of calm began to spread between them. The remnants of the shattered echo, the pull of past lives, had receded—faded into nothingness like a morning mist when the sun rises high enough to burn it away.

The world before them was entirely new, untouched by the passage of time. It was a land unlike anything they had known, a place where the sky seemed to stretch forever, a deep, vivid blue that held no clouds. The wind whispered softly through the leaves of trees they had never seen before, their trunks twisted in a dance of ancient grace. It was as though the world itself was taking a deep breath, waiting for something, something that only they could give it.

Veyrina inhaled deeply, the air filling her lungs with the sweet scent of earth and life—something she hadn't realized she'd missed until now. She could feel the pulse of this new world beneath her feet, the way the ground hummed with a quiet, endless energy.

"This place," Elyndra said, her voice low, as though speaking louder might break the fragile tranquility surrounding them. "It's… beautiful."

"It is," Veyrina agreed, squeezing Elyndra's hand tighter. "It's strange, though. It feels like we've just stepped into something we were meant to be a part of."

And it did. The land before them, the trees, the flowers blooming under their feet—all of it felt as though it had been waiting for them to arrive. There were no boundaries here, no lines that separated time from space. The realm they had escaped was gone, its echoes now but whispers on the wind.

Yet, even as they stood in this perfect silence, there was an undercurrent of unease, a pulse they couldn't ignore. The echoes of their past lives, the memories of those they had once been, still lingered within them, flickering just beneath the surface of their thoughts. At times, Veyrina could almost hear their voices—faint and distant—like a song that didn't quite belong to her, but one she could still feel in the depths of her soul.

She turned her gaze toward Elyndra, meeting her eyes. There, beneath the quiet surface, she could see it—the same traces of lingering doubt that she herself had felt. The echoes of the past were gone, but they were not entirely forgotten. They were part of them now, inextricable, like a melody woven into their very being.

"It's strange," Elyndra said, reading her thoughts with ease, as she often did. "The echoes—they don't haunt me anymore. But I can feel them. Like they're always there, just out of reach.

I hear their whispers when the wind moves through the trees."

Veyrina nodded, brushing a strand of hair from Elyndra's face. "I know. It's like they've become a part of us. A memory we'll carry with us for the rest of our lives, but not one that will torment us anymore."

There was no more wraith chasing them through endless cycles of time, no more gods waiting to strike them down. The realm's crumbling foundation had been held together by their love, and that love had brought them here. To this moment. To this place. A place where time moved forward unbroken, and their future, whatever it might hold, was now theirs to shape.

The horizon before them shifted, the glow of the setting sun bathing the land in a warm, golden hue. The sky above them, once frozen in the stasis of the echo, was now fluid—alive with possibility. A new chapter had begun. But with it, came the knowledge that their love was the key to all they had endured, and that this love, once bound by curse, was now free to breathe and grow, unencumbered by time.

"Do you think…?" Elyndra began, her voice trailing off. She was searching for the words, the ones that had been on her lips since they had first felt the pull of the realm's unraveling.

Veyrina turned to face her fully, her eyes soft with under-standing. "Do I think what?"

"Do you think we can truly forget everything that happened? The echoes? The pain?" Elyndra asked, her gaze unwavering, even as the wind picked up, playing with the strands of her hair. "I know we're free now. But can we leave the past behind?"

The question lingered in the space between them, a delicate weight neither of them was ready to release.

Veyrina thought for a moment, then smiled—a soft, gentle curve of her lips, as if she had come to an understanding only now. "We can't leave the past behind, Elyndra. Not entirely. It's woven into who we are. The love we fought for, the choices we made—it's all a part of our story. Our history." She looked at their joined hands, then back up at Elyndra, her eyes intense with the certainty of everything they had been through. "But we can choose how we carry it. We don't have to let it define us. We don't have to let it weigh us down. We can let it be a part of us, something we embrace, something we use to build the future."

Elyndra's gaze softened, and for the first time since they had stepped into this world, Veyrina saw the weight she carried— lighten. It was a moment of clarity, of peace. The echoes would always be with them. But they no longer had the power to bind them, to tear them apart.

"This world," Elyndra whispered, looking out at the horizon once more, "it's… new. And I know we can make it our own. But what if… what if the past comes for us again? What if the echoes rise up and try to claim us again?"

Veyrina stepped closer, wrapping her arms around Elyndra, pulling her close. "We won't let it. We've faced the worst that could come, together. We've already broken the curse, already defeated the gods. What else is there? Our love is stronger than anything the past can throw at us."

Elyndra leaned into her, resting her head on Veyrina's shoulder, feeling the steady beat of her heart. It was a sound that grounded her, reminded her of everything they had overcome, everything they had fought for. The land around them shimmered in the fading light, like a reflection of their own journey—a journey that had brought them to this very moment.

"I think I'm finally beginning to believe that," Elyndra

murmured, her voice full of emotion.

Veyrina kissed the top of her head gently. "We don't need to forget the past. We only need to remember that we have each other. And as long as we do, the echoes will never have the power to take us back."

They stood there for a long time, in the embrace of the setting sun, watching as the land before them seemed to breathe. The echoes—those whispers of past lives—began to fade, no longer as loud or as insistent. They had found their peace. A new future stretched out before them, full of unknowns, full of hope, full of possibilities.

And for the first time in what felt like forever, they had no fear. The world was open to them, a canvas yet to be painted. Together.

As the sun finally dipped below the horizon, casting its last rays across the field, Veyrina and Elyndra walked forward, hand in hand. The echoes of their past lives still lingered— gentle, quiet—but they no longer haunted them. Instead, they became a quiet reminder of the love they had fought for, the bond that had withstood the test of time, the curse, and the gods.

Their love had endured through it all.

And now, it would echo forever.

The land stretched out before them, vast and wild, but more importantly, it felt like home. Veyrina and Elyndra walked hand-in-hand, the soft crunch of grass beneath their feet providing a steady rhythm to their steps. The sky was painted in shades of lavender and amber, the sun's final glow casting an ethereal light over the horizon. It was a world unburdened by the weight of time, untouched by the endless cycles of the echo.

Elyndra squeezed Veyrina's hand, drawing her attention to the landscape around them. The towering trees, their branches heavy with unknown fruit, rustled gently in the breeze. Flowers of every color—some that neither woman had ever seen, nor could name—lined their path, blooming in vibrant hues that shimmered in the fading light.

"Do you feel it?" Elyndra asked softly, her voice filled with wonder.

Veyrina nodded, a smile tugging at her lips. "Yes, I do. It's like… the land itself is alive, breathing with us. It's a place of new beginnings."

They had fought for this—fought for their freedom from the echo and its suffocating grip on their lives. They had faced unimaginable trials, but now, standing here, the weight of it all seemed to dissolve. The past, with its ghosts and gods, had no hold over them anymore. Their love was their own, no longer bound by fate or time. It was a love that had transcended every boundary, every restriction.

Veyrina glanced sideways at Elyndra, noticing the way the soft light seemed to embrace her, the warmth of the sun playing across her face. It was as though the world itself recognized the strength of their bond, honoring it in this quiet, peaceful moment.

"I never thought we would get here," Elyndra admitted, her voice barely above a whisper. "I never thought we'd be free."

Veyrina's heart swelled at the words, her love for Elyndra overflowing. "We're free because we chose to be. Together."

Elyndra smiled, her eyes meeting Veyrina's with a depth that spoke of all they had been through, all they had survived. "Together," she echoed, the word a promise, a vow.

The silence between them was not heavy, nor laden with unspoken fears. It was peaceful—one that enveloped them in warmth and understanding, a quiet acknowledgment that the future was theirs to shape, free from the constraints of what had come before.

The land ahead of them beckoned—a new world, unmarked by the past, waiting for them to discover it. Veyrina and Elyndra continued forward, their footsteps light, as though the earth itself was welcoming them home. The world they had left behind—the realm they had shattered—was fading, its echo now a distant memory. And though the memories of their past lives would always be a part of them, they no longer held the power to dictate their fate.

At the edge of the horizon, the first stars began to twinkle, the sky growing darker with the promise of nightfall. The two women paused, turning their eyes upward to where the heavens stretched endlessly above them. For the first time, the sky felt infinite—an expanse where anything was possible, where time was no longer their enemy.

"We'll make this world our own," Elyndra whispered, her voice full of resolve. "No more echoes, no more gods. Just us. And the love we've fought for."

Veyrina turned to her, the smile on her lips tender but fierce. "Together. Always."

And in that moment, as the last rays of the sun faded behind them and the stars lit up the sky, they both knew—truly knew—that they had found something eternal.

The love they shared, the bond that had survived the test of time, had not only saved them but had saved the world they now stood in. The echoes of the past, though forever a part of them, were no longer a force that could divide them. Instead, they had become a reminder—a symbol of the trials they had faced, and the strength they had found within each other.

The stars above them seemed to shimmer with the same quiet understanding, a silent witness to the journey they had undertaken. There was no more fear, no more hesitation. Only the certainty that, no matter what lay ahead, they would face it together.

Veyrina took a deep breath, feeling the cool night air fill her lungs. For the first time in what felt like an eternity, she felt at peace. And when she turned to Elyndra, she saw the same calm reflected in her eyes.

"Let's walk," Veyrina said, her voice steady and full of promise.

They began to walk again, side by side, the land opening up before them like a canvas ready to be painted with the colors of their future. The echoes of the past, the love, the loss, the battles—they were all behind them now, woven into the fabric of their souls, but no longer a chain. They were free to live, free to choose.

And as the night unfolded around them, they knew this was just the beginning.

Their love would echo through the ages, not as a curse, but as a testament—a beacon of devotion, of sacrifice, of a love that had survived time itself.

Together, they stepped forward into the unknown, their hearts beating in unison, their love the one constant in a world that had no end. The echoes of forever had found their peace, and so had they.

The end.